DEPRESSION:
The Blue Plague

Current surveys show that, over the past few decades, cases of self-poisoning admitted to an Edinburgh hospital have increased dramatically from approximately 50 a year to 1,300 a year. Similarly, a fifth of all medical admissions to a Leicester hospital are cases of attempted suicide.

Behind these appalling statistics lurks a problem commonplace in every doctor's surgery and familiar to almost every family at some time or another—DEPRESSION. The nature and degree of anguish caused by this 'Blue Plague' is often not appreciated by the sufferer's family, or even by the family doctor. Suicide itself is simply the final act of desperation.

Essentially, Dr. Watt's book is a guide through the often unknown territory of mental illness, with special reference to depression. The book is recommended by Professor Clarke, President of the Royal College of Physicians, London, in the following terms:

'With great expertise, the author has produced a book of interest to experienced consultants and general practitioners, and at the same time informative to—and easily understood by—paramedical staff and the lay public'.

Any man's death diminishes *me*,
because I am involved in *mankind*;
And therefore never send
to know for whom the *bell* tolls;
It tolls for *thee*.

John Donne

PRIORY EDITORIAL CONSULTANTS

THE CARE AND WELFARE LIBRARY

Consultant Medical Editor: Alexander R. K. Mitchell
MB, ch.B, MRCPE, MRCPsych.

DEPRESSION: THE BLUE PLAGUE

C. A. H. WATTS

OBE, MD, FRCPG

Foreword by
EMERITUS PROFESSOR C. A. CLARKE
CBE, MD, FRS

President of the Royal College of Physicians, London

PRIORY PRESS LIMITED

The Care and Welfare Library

SBN 85078 107 8 (Paperback)
      85078 106 X (Hardback)
Copyright © 1973 by C. A. H. Watts
First published in 1973 by
Priory Press Limited
101 Grays Inn Road London WC1
Made and printed in Great Britain by
The Garden City Press Limited
Letchworth, Hertfordshire SG6 1JS

Contents

Foreword

by

Emeritus Professor C. A. Clarke, CBE, MD, FRS, President of the
Royal College of Physicians, London.

DR. WATTS is a general practitioner in the village of Ibstock,
Leicestershire, and has for many years been particularly interested in the psychological illnesses of his patients. Here he tells
us of his experiences in this specialty, with "Blue Plague"—
depression—being the chief enemy.

The author sees the problem not only in its present-day setting
but in the history of man's evolution. He fully appreciates that
anxiety and mood swings originally had great survival value, but
interestingly they seem to have become pathological with the
advance of civilization, and there is no doubt that affluence as
such does not bring peace of mind. Because of their origins,
depressions and anxiety will never be conquered, but their effects
can be greatly alleviated with modern methods of treatment. Dr.
Watts not only deals with these, but gives us in addition the
points of view of patients, the role of relatives, of the community,
of health visitors and of the social workers. With great expertise,
the author has produced a book of interest to experienced consultants and general practitioners, and at the same time informative to—and easily understood by—paramedical staff and
the lay public.

It will be seen therefore that the author has combined a
description of clinical skills with that of the organizations necessary
to back them up, and two things stand out in his approach. One
is that patients are his prime concern, and the short case histories
with which the book abounds keep up the reader's interest, and

moreover they emphasize that administration, though important, is of secondary consideration. The other is that he has demonstrated that it is perfectly possible to describe organizational details in comprehensible English, in marked contrast to the opaqueness which characterizes so many official documents on the subject.

As a Leicester man, I am proud to see this contribution from my county to a most important current medical problem.

C. A. Clarke

March, 1973

Acknowledgements

IN writing a book of this nature, the author is indebted to many people who have inspired or helped him in its creation.

Dr. Paul Rowntree started the ball rolling when he invited me to give the 1971 Oration to the York Medical Society. I chose as my title for this address "The Blue Plague." My views on the use of drugs were given a rude shaking by Dr. Peter Parish who allowed me to read over the manuscript of his M.D. thesis. The Journal of the Royal College of General Practitioners agreed to publish an abbreviated version of my oration, and this paper caught the keen publishing eye of Dr. Geoffrey Eley. He invited me to enlarge on my thesis, and this is just what I have done in this small book.

I have trespassed on the territory of other workers such as the district nurses, health visitors and trained social workers of all kinds. Many of these people helped me considerably, it would be impossible to name them all. I must acknowledge the special help given by Miss Grace Axton, Miss Doris West, Mrs. Marie Tebbutt, and Mrs. Ann Connon. Without their help and suggestions the chapters on their disciplines would have been very difficult to produce; at the same time I take full responsibility for what has been written. It is obvious from many of the case histories how indebted I am to my fellow general practitioners. I would like to thank Dr. Geoffrey Eley of Priory Press for all his suggestions and continued encouragement. Also, my thanks are due to Mrs. B. L. Gretton for the unstinting help she gave with the typing.

I am particularly indebted to Professor C. Astley Clarke for reading the manuscript and agreeing to write the Foreword, all this in the middle of his term of office as President of the Royal

9

College of Physicians. I would like also to thank him for all the moral support he has given to my work in Ibstock.

I will ever be grateful to the people of Ibstock who have for so long been such good and loyal patients. Last, but by no means least, I must acknowledge the help given to me by my wife Dr. Betty Watts. She was, in fact, a complete partner in this enterprise but she is too modest to admit to this role.

Ibstock, Leicestershire, 1973

I

The Problem

HOMO sapiens, as his name implies, is the most intelligent creature to inhabit this earth of ours. In an incredibly short time he has emerged from a primitive state in which he had to struggle to survive. He had to hunt for food, find shelter for himself and his family, and he had to protect his small tribal unit from animal predators and men of other territories who sought to kill or dispossess him. It was a hard and precarious life with an endless struggle to exist, much as the Bushman survives in the Kalahari desert today.

From the start of the early Neolithic settlements the rate of evolution in terms of creature comfort and social amenities was extremely slow. Indeed, this simple life persisted until comparatively recent times. Only 200 years ago the native Irish and the Highland Scots lived in near stone age conditions except for their chiefs. Life was every bit as hard as that of the primeval farmers of 5,000 years before.

With the industrial revolution which began in the eighteenth century things began to move and changes have proceeded at an ever increasing pace. Today Western man suddenly finds himself living in the modern world of high speed travel and communications, of enormous and complicated societies and concrete jungles. Well over half the people in developed countries today live in towns of more than 20,000 inhabitants, half of them in cities of more than half a million people. Enormous conurbations of over 7 million inhabitants, like London, New York and Tokyo, are growing at twice the speed of smaller cities.[1] Wealth has increased enormously since World War II and most Western nations enjoy unheard of prosperity. For the first time in his long history of

[1] Leach, Gerald, *The Biocrats* (Penguin Books, 1972).

about 250,000 years Western man finds himself no longer pain-
fully aware of poverty and death by starvation. There is more
than enough for everyone, while unbelievable luxuries are thrown
in for good measure.

The intellectual and anatomical make up of man has changed
very little in the past few thousand years. He has had to learn to
adjust to changing circumstances, but his basic and instinctive
reactions remain closely related to those of the higher animals.

A cat sitting on the doorstep in the sun sleeps peacefully. The
moment it hears, sees, or smells an approaching dog it becomes
alerted so that it can give battle or scramble up the nearest tree.
This alerting mechanism is very rapid. The smell or sound of the
dog sends a message to the brain, which passes an alarm signal
to the adrenal glands. Adrenalin is rapidly passed into the blood
stream. The pulse rate is increased, sugar is liberated from the
liver into the blood, the pupils dilate, the hair is erected and the
whole organism is placed in a state of maximum efficiency in a
split second. If the cat had not been endowed with this remarkable mechanism, it would never have survived. Our cave-man
ancestors relied on this self-same built-in protective device, which
was essential to him, surrounded as he was by possible enemies
or predators.

Modern man is rarely confronted by sudden dangers of this
kind. A country girl walking across a field might possibly hear
something which makes her look over her shoulder to see a bull
bearing down on her. Her fear or "fight flight" reaction comes
to her rescue. She races to the stile at a speed she could never
normally achieve : she leaps it like an expert hurdler, something
she would never have attempted under ordinary circumstances.
She finds herself in the lane, breathless but unharmed. She meets
a friend who at once says, "What on earth is the matter—you
look dreadful!" Her face is pale and sweating, her pupils are
dilated, her pulse is racing, and if she but knew it her hair would
be erected, all by the self-same safety mechanism shown by the
cat. The fact that she feels queer and looks strange does not
surprise her. She knows she has had a bad fright and is only
thankful that she was able to react so successfully. Whether she

attributes her escape to angels or her adrenals depends on the extent of her scientific education.

This situation only rarely arises in the modern world. People are seldom suddenly placed in such peril, but they are prone to worry and be anxious in our complex modern society.

Anxiety is, in fact, the same kind of emotion as fear only it is less dramatic in onset. Basically anxiety, like fear, is a useful protective mechanism. The mother who notices her small boy is feverish and ill tucks the youngster up in bed, and keeps a watchful eye on him. If the invalid does not improve her anxiety prompts her to send for the doctor, and to place the onus on him to get her child well again. The mother's anxiety is a protective device for the child. The good mother does not wait for accidents to happen to her toddler : she uses all her imagination to remove objects which could be dangerous. All medicines and tablets are locked away, out of reach of the child. The shallow fish pond on the lawn is securely netted so that the child cannot possibly fall into the water and be drowned. The anxiety of the orator or the athlete is necessary to produce maximum efficiency. The speaker who is glib and over-relaxed, claiming that he finds public speaking no strain at all, is likely to bore everyone but himself. Some degree of stage fright is a necessity to a good performance.

Anxiety, or the closely allied feeling of frustration, can effect nations as well as individuals. Desperate situations often provoke ingenuity and invention. When Islamic armies blocked the caravan route to the Orient, the sailors of Europe were spurred into epic voyages which took them round the Cape of Good Hope and across the Atlantic in an attempt to find a new way to the East. In the same way World War II saw the perfection of jet propulsion for aircraft, scientists worked overtime to facilitate the mass production of penicillin to help the wounded, and advances in nuclear physics produced the atomic bomb.

Some anxiety is inescapable for an intelligent and imaginative creature such as man, especially when he is forced to live in our modern complex world, and it cannot always lead to useful activities such as those of the mother who used her imagination to protect her child. But Homo sapiens is a resilient animal and a modicum of "free anxiety," that is anxiety which is not put to some useful purpose, usually does no harm. It is only when it occurs in overwhelming proportions that it becomes dangerous and an illness.

Every man has his breaking point if the anxiety is severe enough or lasts too long. The British swimming team did not do very well in the 1972 Olympics. On a television interview their coach said he thought that the intense nervous strain of the situation was too much for them, and they could not maintain their own best standards. David Wilkie who won a silver medal had the necessary resources to go in and swim his best. Similarly, a highly strung housewife with four small children was able to cope with all her problems pretty well until her husband was killed in an accident. This sudden and overwhelming strain was too much for her and she went to pieces. For several weeks she was completely unable to cope with the situation.

Anxiety has the same effect upon the body as fear, so the anxious person keeps overproducing adrenalin. Her pulse quickens and she becomes conscious of her heart beating. This causes a wave of secondary anxiety, and so a vicious circle is set up. Anxiety increases the pulse rate, giving rise to fear, which increases the pulse rate still further, creating yet more fear. The original worry is forgotten. Only the rapid pulse and sense of constriction in the chest occupy the consciousness and the victim assumes she is having a heart attack. The girl who escaped the bull had the same sensations, but they did not worry her because she knew why her pulse was racing. The anxious person does not associate the real problem with the symptoms, nor does the increased amount of adrenalin available to her help her to solve her problems or serve any obviously useful purpose. The victim of pathological anxiety lives in a state of tension, jumps at the least unexpected sound, tends to be very body conscious. Problems, real or imaginary, keep going round and round in her mind. Such anxiety has been described as "circular waves of futile thought beating up against a pillar of fear."

Anxiety is one of the most common emotions to find a place in our human make up. A second emotion called depression is almost as common, and depression is the essential ingredient of the blue plague. Anxiety can in certain circumstances give rise to depression. The mother who was worried about her child and called in the doctor, breaks down and cries when she is told the child must go to hospital. She sees, as it were, a red light, her child is very ill, perhaps in danger of his life. The original anxiety is augmented by depression. There are, of course, many other sources of depression and these will be discussed in another chapter.

The more intelligent mammals can show signs of depression as well as those of anxiety. In the absence of a beloved master a dog can go off her food, become fretful and obviously unhappy. Konrad Lorenz[2] describes a bitch of his whose behaviour became quite abnormal and impossible when he had to leave the animal to join the army. So depraved were her habits she had to be segregated in a strong pen. After three months he had leave and returned home. The bitch did not recognize him when she saw him, but rushed towards him growling aggressively. When she smelt him, however, she stopped and her raised crest subsided. She pricked up her ears, her back legs gave way, she sat down and raised her head in the air and then for half a minute howled like a wolf. Her cry over, like a thunderbolt she greeted her master and became a normal well-behaved dog once more.

Although fretful behaviour is common in animals and demonstrates their suffering and distress, Homo sapiens is the only animal who will kill himself when depressed. Lemmings are drowned by the thousand when they migrate across fiords or into the open sea, but this is not suicide in the human sense.

Depression in its medical setting is a distressing lowering of mental and physical vitality. It is not as easy to explain as anxiety. Many who suffer from depression are active extroverts who can often do the work of two people, and it has been suggested that depression is nature's way of compelling these people to cut down their activities. This explanation is by no means as convincing or as clear as that of the function of anxiety. The

2 Lorenz, Konrad, *Man Meets Dog* (Penguin Books, 1964).

latter serves as a useful alerting mechanism : depression is retarding but it is difficult to imagine that this is its function.

How far depression was prevalent among our early ancestors is not possible to say, but suicide has occurred ever since history was recorded. The affluence of modern society has not eased the situation. When Harold Macmillan was premier in Britain he told us the man in the street had never had it so good, but in that year well over 5,000 people took their own lives. The country is undoubtedly enjoying a vastly improved standard of living with far better health than previous generations experienced. This is reflected in the improved weight and height of the children. The expectation of life has indeed improved and a child born today has a very good chance of drawing his old age pension. In spite of more wealth, possessions, better food and physical health, there are cogent signs that we live in an unhappy and insecure society. The suicide rate remains far too high. There has been a drop in the figures over the past few years but authorities like Stengel suggest the fall is spurious. The coroner in England and the procurator fiscal in Scotland bend over backwards to bring in any verdict other than suicide. Stengel quoted this report,[3] "A man who hanged himself in his cell in Walton Prison made a suicidal gesture and not a deliberate attempt on his life, and accidentally killed himself, the coroner Mr. A. B. said yesterday— The prison doctor said that the dead man was given to histrionic displays. Some months previously he had inflicted a wound on his wrist, and said he wanted to take his life." One of my own patients who had had three periods in hospital for depression and was known to be suicidal, was found drowned in a foot of water. The verdict of accidental death was returned as the woman had left no note or given any clear indication of her intent. With cases such as this in mind one can have little faith in the validity of the figures for suicide, but nevertheless the suicide rate is one of the few figures we have with which to measure the ebb and flow of depression in the community. What is obvious

[3] Stengel, E., Presidential Address to Sixth International Conference on Suicide Prevention (1971).

today is that material prosperity and fame does not ensure happiness.

Successful suicide itself is only the visible tip of an iceberg of depression. For every success there are some ten to twenty attempts. On the whole the suicide rate has remained fairly static since the war, but the figures for attempts by self poisoning have gone up at an astronomical rate. To quote just two examples, the admission rate of poisoned patients at the Edinburgh Royal Infirmary from 1930 to 1950 was between 50 and 100 cases per annum, but in 1960 there were about 350 cases, and in 1970 almost 1,300 such cases[4]; while suicide attempts accounted for 18.9 per cent of all medical admissions to the Leicester Royal Infirmary,[5] and it was indeed the commonest cause for a medical admission. It is estimated that over 70,000 cases may be admitted to hospitals in the United Kingdom each year.

A further index of social unrest and unhappiness is a veritable tidal wave of addiction to alcohol and to drugs, both hard and soft, and experts have estimated that one per cent of the adult population of the country is seriously addicted to alcohol. In England and Wales there are about 36 million people of seventeen and over, so we must have some 360,000 addicts, which is a larger number than all the psychiatric hospital beds in the community. The drug problem, while not so enormous, is growing and is much more evident in towns and cities than in rural areas.

Suicide, self poisoning, and addiction are all major symptoms of dissatisfaction and unhappiness in the community, and quite apart from extremes such as this, vast numbers of people are turning for comfort to tranquillizers, sedatives and hypnotics which they can, in many cases, obtain from their family doctors with the greatest ease. These are often dispensed in such large quantities one gets the impression that such generous prescriptions are a means of keeping a tiresome patient away from the consulting room. Some people take a benign view of pill con-

[4] Matthew, H., *Update*, August 1971, p. 947.
[5] Ellis, G. G., Cornish, K. A. and Hewer, R. L. (1966), *The Practitioner*, **196**, 557.

suming habits as long as there is no constant escalation of the dose. It has been suggested in fact that middle aged women take their sleeping tablets in much the same way as their husbands have night caps.

In addition, there is a vast amount of self medication going on in the community, bought freely across the counter from any chemist or herbalist.

The "Blues" or the "Blue Plague" is certainly a major problem of our time. There has always been human suffering, physical, mental and social, and there have always been bodies like the Churches, or people like William Wilberforce, the Quakers of York headed by the Tukes, and David Livingstone who have been in the forefront of the battle in an attempt to relieve it. Today when the plague has reached epidemic proportions only about ten per cent of the population go to church.

The problem is immense. It is a social sickness, and not just a medical problem, and this really is the basic reason for writing this book. It is an attempt to show how each section of the community has a part to play in finding a solution.

What is Depression?

THERE is often a good deal of confusion in people's minds as to what is really meant by depressive illness. A good definition of depression in a medical sense is the lowering of mental and physical vitality to the point of distress.

There are different types of depression and many causes, and in one form or another most people experience something of this unpleasant syndrome. It can be a simple response to many adverse circumstances which vary from such mundane events as the arrival of mother-in-law for a holiday, or the receipt of an income tax demand, to the profound crisis of life such as the loss of a spouse.

These downward swings of mood are, of course, in a way counterbalanced by the upward swings caused by good news, falling in love or winning the pools, but for the greater part of his life a man's mood hovers around a norm. This is comparable with the slight swing of normal body temperature. In excessive heat sweating and evaporation cause heat loss and in cold weather shivering produces heat. Both mechanisms help to maintain the temperature around 37.0°C (98.4° F), but there is a slight but distinct physiological swing above and below this mark. This state of bodily equilibrium is known as homeostasis.

The control mechanism for temperature is in a part of the brain called the hypothalamus, and this control can fail under certain circumstances. An infection such as tonsilitis or measles upsets the mechanism and the victim is then said to run a fever. This fever deviation is, of course, a very common symptom of human illness. On the other hand, the body can be cooled too far, as it may be with a walker on a mountain who is inadequately protected and gets lost when the clouds come down. If the body temperature falls below 30°C, the victim is likely to become comatose, and death can supervene if the body temperature sinks much lower, or the exposure lasts too long.

The same part of the brain, the hypothalamus, has other centres which control such things as appetite, and mood. The latter, the emotional control centre, is the mechanism that keeps a man's emotional tone at a fairly even level, but, as with temperature, there is a physiological swing. Some mornings we wake up excited if there is a treat in store, while on Monday mornings we are not so cheerful with the prospect of a whole working week ahead of us.

Just as the body's thermostat can be upset by infectious illness or extreme cold, so the emotional control centre can be upset by various agents. Before the Second World War one frequently saw infants suffering from what was called "pink disease." Their skin was flushed and red, particularly on the palms of their hands and the soles of their feet, which gave the disease its name, but the predominant and distressing symptom was their utter misery. These babies were very restless and cried constantly. The cause was eventually traced to teething powders popular at the time which were found to contain small quantities of mercury, added to alleviate constipation. This metal acted upon the emotional control centre of the brain, producing a depression which could last for weeks or even months after the use of powders had been discontinued. Since this element has been excluded from teething powders pink disease has disappeared.

We now know there are a number of drugs which act in a similar way with adults. Reserpine and some of the drugs used to lower blood pressure can cause quite severe symptoms of depression which can last long after the drug has been stopped. The contraceptive pill in some women causes depression. There are, of course, also drugs which can elate the mood, of which the best known is the amphetamine group including dexedrine and the "purple hearts" so popular with addicts. Alcohol can work both ways. In the first instance it makes the drinker relaxed and merry, and some people even when very drunk can exude a peculiar cheerfulness. The aftermath is depression, commonly called a hangover, and it may be accompanied by a severe head-ache and other distressing symptoms.

All of these drugs act on the Emotional Control Centre in the brain, as, indeed, do any factors which cause depression.

THE REACTIVE DEPRESSION

Adverse circumstances are probably the most common cause of depression and depression caused in this way is said to be reactive. Many instances spring to mind, and it can occur at any age. The infant, who for some reason or another is separated from his mother, is likely to get depressed and can indeed become as ill as a child with chemically induced "pink disease." Bowlby[1] describes what happens to a young child from fifteen to thirty months separated from his mother in three phases of Protest, Despair, and Detachment. "At first with tears and anger he demands his mother back and seems hopeful that he will succeed in getting her. This phase of Protest may last several days. Later he becomes quieter but to the discerning eye it is clear that much as ever he remains preoccupied with his absent mother and still yearns for her return, but his hopes have faded and he is in the phase of Despair. Eventually, however, a greater change occurs. He seems to forget his mother so that when she comes for him he remains curiously uninterested in her, and may even seem not to recognise her. This is the phase of Detach-ment. In each of these phases the child is prone to tantrums and episodes of destructive behaviour often of a disquietingly violent kind." Bowlby likens separation from the mother to a process of mourning, and this concept was certainly recognized by the French who coined the aphorism, "Partir c'est mourir un peu." To say goodbye is to die a little.

Going to school may well cause a violent upset in the child who both dislikes his new environment and yearns to be back at home with mother. If there is a baby at home, fears that the younger sibling is getting too much attention may fan the flames.

[1] Bowlby, J. (1961). *American Journal of Psychiatry*, **118,** 481.

Depression: The Blue Plague

In older children the emergence of overt sexual life may cause great concern. With better sex education this problem is probably less hurtful than it used to be when girls were merely told they were "poorly" during menstruation, and boys were warned that masturbation caused all kinds of fearful ills culminating in insanity if the wicked habit could not be mastered.

Broken love affairs are a very common cause of deep depression, and many a lover has threatened to take his life if his love goes unrequited. Some people who have been jilted do just that. It is a very effective way of incurring pity and punishing the faithless party.

It is hardly necessary to explain to a jilted lover the cause of his depression. On the other hand the reason for the symptoms may be obvious to an observer, but, for one reason or another, obscured from the patient himself. A young husband with an unfaithful wife may be the last person to realize what is going on. Any suspicion of her behaviour is so painful it is repressed, pushed out of the conscious mind into the subconscious. Like some deep hidden abscess it causes painful symptoms, but other things are blamed and the real cause of the trouble is evaded. Very often neither the observer nor the patient is aware of the real trouble and the basic cause may only become evident when the patient has complete confidence in the person who is trying to help him, and is able freely to discuss his hopes and fears.

A man aged twenty-four came to see me complaining of pains in his chest. He was a commercial traveller and had been married for just six months. He was very worried about himself and was sure he had a bad heart. The pain had started in the train on the way home from a trip which had kept him in Scotland for several days. There was no evidence of any heart disease and I was quite sure the basis of his trouble was worry. Once I had won his confidence he told me about his work, and how much he hated having to leave his new wife for days on end, but the money was good, and he could not afford to change his job. He went on to say that when last away from home he had probably drunk too much, especially among a certain circle of friends. He described how the night before his "heart attack" he had been to a wild party and had got very drunk. He was not sure but it was just possible he had seduced one of the girls at the party, but he could not remember. Then the picture became clear. He obviously had been unfaithful to his wife, and he had done his best to repress the memory of the act. However, forgetting his misdemeanour did not entirely remove his sense of guilt which had emerged as a fear of heart disease. In the first instance this trick of his mind was useful. When he met his wife and told her of his pain, she was as kind and loving as a wife could be, a reception very different to the one he deserved. However, in the end the bargain was a bad one. The obsession about his heart made him an invalid and his life a misery. He had exchanged a guilty conscience for the fear of heart disease and sudden death, and it was only when he was able to accept all the implications of what had happened that recovery was possible.

DEPRESSION DUE TO PHYSICAL ILLNESSES

All physical diseases carry with them a psychological component. A few, like pulmonary tuberculosis, sometimes used to cause a strange euphoria or elevation of spirits but usually illness is depressing. It is rarely comfortable or convenient to be ill, although there are times when an illness can free a person from unwelcome obligations for a while. The common cold can make the sufferer pretty miserable and may put him into a state of indecision. Should he go to work to save inconvenience at the office, or will he infect the whole staff and make himself really ill in the process? This is a very mildly depressing situation in which everyone of us finds himself from time to time.

There are, however, a number of illnesses which can produce quite a profound state of depression which can last long after the illness itself has gone. All the virus diseases like influenza and infective hepatitis can cause depression. I was once looking after an old man of seventy who had a typical attack of influenza in an epidemic. When the fever had gone his spirits remained very low. I noticed in the evening paper a short announcement to the effect that he had been left £3,000 by a relative who had died and I expected that when I saw him again this would have cheered him up and helped his recovery. He was, however, still very miserable and had no interest in his windfall. It was several weeks before he became himself again, and was able to enjoy life and his good fortune.

There are many other organic diseases and deficiencies which can cause depression. Patients suffering from diabetes, anaemia or nephritis may become depressed and this may well be the symptom which sends the patient to the doctor. Many years ago now, I was asked to see a man who was indeed very depressed and he had suicidal ideas. In those days the only available treatment was in a mental hospital, and he refused to go to such a place. He was seen by a psychiatrist who endorsed my diagnosis, but neither the patient nor his family would consent to hospital treatment. For some eighteen months the man was seen at regular intervals and it was a thankless task, but at last he consented to go to hospital. There it was found he was suffering from hitherto unsuspected pernicious anaemia and he was given injections of liver extract. He made a good and rapid recovery, and is now a fit eighty year old who has had no further symptoms of depression. Similarly, a diabetic whose control has become poor can show many severely depressive symptoms which disappear rapidly when the regime is tightened up and tests improve.

Injury, as well as disease, can affect the emotional centre. I had a patient who was knocked down in a fog and severely concussed. When he recovered from his injuries he remained morose and depressed, quite a different personality. He was awarded generous compensation by the courts but this did not improve his spirits.

Hormones are chemicals which are produced by certain glands and which, circulating in the bloodstream, control some of the vital functions of the body. The most important of these glands are in the ovaries or testes, the adrenal glands above the kidneys, the thyroid gland in the neck, and the small but very important pituitary gland which lies under the brain on the base of the skull. If these glands get out of balance a state of depression may result. It is for this reason that most women have some feeling of tension and depression before the menses and in some this can be quite severe. Dalton[2] has shown that, in women, forty-seven per cent of cases of depression severe enough to be admitted to a mental hospital were admitted during that vulnerable time, and fifty-three per cent of attempted suicides occurred just before or during menstruation. Women also appear to be more accident prone at this time, as fifty-two per cent of accidents occurred during this period.[3]

Having a baby is another critical time in a woman's life, and once again there are big changes in the way the hormones work. The afterbirth, which during pregnancy manufactured some vital chemicals, is voided once the baby has been born, and the ovaries start to resume their normal function. The pituitary gland secretes substances which contract the uterine muscle to prevent bleeding and, at the same time, another hormone works on the breast tissues to produce milk. There is in fact an enormous change of hormone activity. This is, of course, just one factor, but the woman who has had a baby is very prone to depression, and the "fourth day blues" occurs in most women. There are other factors at work at this time to contribute to the depression : physical discomfort, the sickening pain of piles, or breast tension.

There may well also be some reactive depression. For nine whole months the woman has been preparing for her baby. She has collected a layette, she has reorganized the house, she has had to curtail social engagements and put up with a certain amount of physical distortion if not frank discomfort. Few women thoroughly enjoy the last few weeks of pregnancy, and the young mother longs for the day when she has her baby safely in her arms. She builds up an exaggerated idea of how lovely it will be, and when the great day has come and gone, there is a short stage of disillusioment. Her tail is sore, her breasts ache,

[2] Dalton, K. (1959), *British Medical Journal*, **1**, 148.
[3] Dalton, K. (1960). *British Medical Journal*, **2**, 1425.

the baby keeps crying, and she is thoroughly homesick. Surrounded by flowers and the cards of well wishers she feels sad and miserable. She reminds herself how lucky she has been to have such a lovely baby, she feels guilty and ashamed of being tearful and morose, little thinking that most women have this bad patch. Whatever the cause, this phase normally soon passes, and the young mother enjoys her new way of life, in spite of the occasional inconvenience of having to make some adjustment.

Sometimes, however, the depression lingers on for months or even years. It may not be severe, and the mother feels she cannot keep on complaining that she is not really well. Everyone is so kind she must just pull herself together. It is not uncommon in medical practice to meet a woman who admits she has never felt really well since the birth of her last child. A young teacher became obsessed with strange ideas about sex, an obsession which had started after the birth of her second baby. She felt there was something seriously wrong, being unable either to satisfy her husband or be satisfied herself, and she felt miserably unhappy about this state of affairs which had lasted for some eighteen months before she sought advice. She had other symptoms of depression, insomnia, and early morning lethargy, and she was given antidepressant drugs. In two weeks she ceased to worry about her sex problems, and in a month she declared she was back to normal, and she has remained well ever since. But for treatment she could have remained miserable, growing more and more introspective for months or even years.

Very occasionally childbirth precipitates a severe mental breakdown. The mother may be suicidal, or be in danger of injuring her child. This psychotic reaction is uncommon, but it may be so violent and severe as to require treatment in a psychiatric hospital. Happily, the outlook in such cases is extremely good and, however ill the patient may become, complete recovery usually occurs, but there is a danger of recurrence after a subsequent confinement. I remember a mother who had had such a breakdown after the birth of her first child and was extremely apprehensive after the birth of her second baby. All went well until the third week when she developed an infection in one kidney which added a further strain, and in twenty-four hours she was in the throes of a complete mental breakdown. I visited her in hospital and I felt most alarmed and depressed myself, wondering if she could ever recover. However, she did get better after an illness of about three months' duration, and ever since has been mentally completely well, an active happy individual. It is worth noting that the acute and sudden mental breakdown usually does far better than the illness which has a slow and insidious onset. This knowledge can be a great comfort to relatives who are naturally dreadfully alarmed and worried by the unexpected illness which so often needs to be treated in a psychiatric hospital.

In the 1920s the term "involutional melancholia" was coined. It was felt that depression at the menopause was a different illness from depression at other times in life. This concept is questioned by most doctors today, but with the cessation of the menses the possibility of further pregnancies ceases and there is a big change in hormonal activity. These factors make the menopausal woman more vulnerable than other age groups. Depression is indeed very common at this time of life and the label of "melancholia" has the additional merit of retaining in our vocabulary a term which has been in use since the time of Hippocrates four centuries before the birth of Christ.

ENDOGENOUS DEPRESSION

This term means depression which comes from within. It is, in fact, a disorder of the emotional control centre for which we can see no obvious cause, and many patients suffering from this type of depression show a dramatic response to physical methods of treatment.

The middle aged housewife wringing her hands may say "I have a fine husband, three lovely children, a beautiful home, I have everything I want, but I am utterly miserable." A hard-working conscientious type of person suddenly, without any cause, finds himself drained of energy and unable to cope with problems and a routine which he could normally manage "standing on his head."

A young "up and coming" business executive came to see me perplexed and very worried about himself. He had always enjoyed his work and felt completely on top of his job until a few weeks before, since when he had found himself less and less able to cope. He believed himself to be in danger of losing his job because he realized that the quality of his work was declining and he was unable to explain why. He had other symptoms which suggested he was suffering from endogenous depression, so I started him off on medical treatment. I warned him he would not improve all at once, and that it took the tablets ten to fourteen days to be effective. He reacted with profound relief to the suggestion that he stay away from work. I saw him twice weekly after this and for two weeks there was virtually no change. On the fourteenth day he began to improve, and by the eighteenth day he was delighted with himself and asked to go back to work. I then saw him at weekly intervals. He told me on his next visit he was completely back to normal and had never enjoyed his work more. His only worry was what would happen when he stopped taking tablets!

In some ways a person with this type of depression can be likened to a woman who has become very anaemic because she she has been losing more blood from her menses than she has been able to replace in her diet. The result is that she is very pale, is short of energy, and becomes breathless on exertion. This woman's body is crying out for one simple chemical—iron. If she is given some iron preparation in a matter of four to six weeks all her symptoms will disappear and she will return to normal. With certain types of endogenous depression there seems to be some chemical upset or deficiency in brain metabolism and, if this can be corrected by replacing the missing chemical substances, brain function returns to normal. The patient is freed from his depression and other symptoms and he can resume normal work, just as the anaemic woman's healthy colour returns as soon as her body has had time to use the iron to make good the haemoglobin deficiency.

Patients suffering from endogenous depression are often very perplexed by what has happened to them. "I have no pains, I have no worry, but I feel awful, I just cannot understand myself," is one way of expressing their feelings. One woman told her doctor, "There is nothing wrong with my organs, it is just what holds me together which is missing."[4] I tell such patients that the mind is behaving rather like a television set which is out of focus : there is a blurring snow-storm effect and the images are so distorted that it is a pain and a grief to watch the screen. One small twist of the right knob and a clear picture emerges which can be enjoyed. The mind in depression seems to have a block somewhere so that only unpleasant thoughts and messages come through. The birds no longer sing, the sun does not shine, the colour has gone out of life, and everything appears a drab grey. A depressed doctor, who lived in delightful border country and usually thoroughly appreciated it, told me that, when he was depressed, he could look at the most lovely view in his locality and it gave him no pleasure. The realization of this defect really hurt him.

Endogenous depression is far more common than most people realize. It is frequently overlooked, and yet it causes an immense amount of human suffering, both for the patient and the patient's family. This kind of depression is simple to treat once it has been recognized, but if missed, months or even years of invalidism may result, or the patient may end it all in suicide. This is a tragic waste of life, especially as so many of these people are hardworking conscientious types, and most could be helped to recovery if only they are correctly diagnosed and treated.

So, broadly speaking, there are three types of depression, the reactive depression brought on by adverse circumstances, the depression secondary to some physical disease or deficiency, and the endogenous depression with no obvious cause which responds to physical treatment.

To these one could add a fourth type, the congenital pessimist who invariably looks on the black side and always expects trouble. The melancholy Jaques in *As You Like It* was such a

[4] Horder, J. P. (1970). *Personal communication.*

29

one, philosophizing aloud to himself as he watched the wounded deer, its tears falling into the brook. "Poor deer," quoth he, "thou make'st a testament as the worldlings do, giving thy sum of more to that which hath too much." The animal had been separated from the herd and was alone, so Jaques went on, " 'Tis right: thus misery doth part the flux of company." Everyone must know of people who never seem able even to smile, who are always grousing, always miserable, and this attitude of mind indeed cuts them off from the flux of company, as few can put up with their complaining attitude.

To complicate matters further, it is possible to have a mixture of any or all of these four types. Adverse circumstances may complicate a recovery from influenza, and these may both occur at the menopause, a period of hormonal imbalance. There is no guarantee that chronically miserable and pessimistic characters should not have a virus infection or lose a spouse, or even avoid being affected by a genuine endogenous depression. Further, it is not possible to say that the simple reactive depression will be necessarily mild, or the endogenous be severe, for they do not follow so simple a pattern. The depression which follows influenza, or a course of serpasil may become so profound as to assume the characteristics of a severe endogenous depression, and physical treatment specific for the latter is necessary to effect recovery.

A brief reference has already been made to an anxious young mother with four children who lost her husband suddenly in an accident and her fuller history also illustrates this point. She was quite naturally heart-broken by the calamity which had befallen her. Here we had a reactive depression following a set of circumstances in which it was difficult to console the victim. There are drugs which can black out sorrow in sleep for a while, but there is nothing but time to ease the anguish of such a tragedy. The injury was too sudden and too severe. After two weeks she became very strange, at times saying her husband was just on holiday, and at other times she threatened to join him and take the children with her. The intolerable grief had changed sorrow into psychosis and she had become so depressed as to be deluded. Delusions are signs of a very severe endogenous depression. She was taken into a mental hospital where she had electroconvulsive therapy (E.C.T.) and recovered. Normal grief is not easy to deal with, but psychotic depression responds to physical treatment, so that the severity of her reaction was, as it were, a blessing in disguise.

Some people like to view the field of depressive illness as a kind of spectrum. The mild reactive depressions are placed at one extreme and the severe psychotic depressions at the other end of the spectrum, with moderate and mixed depressions in the middle. This is a convenient way of looking at the problem, but it is in fact an oversimplification. There are indeed relatively benign cases of endogenous depression that would have to be placed at the mild end of the spectrum, which is not, therefore, entirely made up of reactive cases. The woman described above began with a reactive depression and progressed rapidly towards the severe end of the spectrum. If one can accept it as a rough guide not always accurate, no harm will be done. The main thing is to recognize that the patient is depressed, and if simple listening and advice about obvious problems does not help, then the patient should be referred to a doctor competent to make an accurate diagnosis and give the proper treatment.

It is as if a certain amount of stimulation can be tolerated by the emotional control centre in the brain, but if the trauma is too violent or lasts too long, the depression becomes deep and irreversible. It then runs on for months or even years unless specific treatment is given to break it up. Depression, unlike some other forms of mental illness, does not cause permanent damage or mental deterioration, and in general a person who has been depressed for a very long time can still be expected to make a complete recovery. Forty years ago little could be done, but today fortunately there are very effective treatments available, and this is one of the reasons why recognition and referral of people with this complaint are so very important.

3

The Patient's Angle

THE FIRST ATTACK

Because depressive illness is more common among women (although it can certainly also afflict men) and because it is so cumbersome to write "he or she" and "himself or herself" all the time, I propose to describe symptoms in the following chapters as if the patient were a woman. The theme would obviously be equally applicable to a man.

For a start I want to consider the patient who, for the first time in her life, finds herself experiencing a depressive illness. There is a sense of rather hurt bewilderment, the patient feels ill, but finds it difficult to describe just how she feels, and she cannot understand herself. She tries to carry on as usual, but this is not at all easy. She tends to lack energy and has to drive herself to complete mundane chores she would do without thinking when she was well. She is worried and a bit frightened and certainly irritable, so that she loses her temper at the least thing, snaps at the children, at once realizing that the fault is hers, and so feels guilty and may well dissolve into tears. People begin to notice she is not herself and perhaps ask her what is wrong. She sometimes says she is all right and silences them in that way, or she may try to describe her feelings, perhaps blaming her "nerves." Well-meaning friends tend to agree with her "diagnosis," and then go on to advise her to pull herself together, to snap out of it, and they suggest that with "nerves" only the patient can help herself to get better. This is poor advice and unlikely to help the patient who, after such admonition, feels more guilty and hopeless than ever. She has tried to help herself and failed. She realizes only too well that she must be a very inadequate and stupid person and she decides that in the future she will keep her troubles to herself. She tries to do this with her next kindly neighbour who inquires, and when the latter goes on to say, "Well you don't exactly look a picture of blooming health," the unhappy woman responds with a flood of tears.

The advice to pull oneself together is wrong on two counts. Firstly, the depressed patient, even if the symptoms are mild, is a sick person, and she can no more change her feelings or her mood, than she can lift herself into the air by tugging on her shoe laces. Secondly, the implication is that anxiety, depression, nervous tension and symptoms of this kind are trivial symptoms to be brushed aside as merely figments of the imagination. Nothing could be further from the truth. These symptoms are very real and extremely painful to the sufferer. Depression, even a mild episode, is one of the most unpleasant experiences anyone can have.

Anxiety, too, can be a devastating sensation. There is a mild gnawing ache we all feel in difficult situations, but severe anxiety is much more painful and it can escalate into a terrifying crisis. Doctors are often told about such attacks, they may even be called out to see such patients, but by the time they arrive the violence of the episode has largely passed and they find a rather shaken patient, and family. There is nothing much to demonstrate by way of physical illness, and the doctor, I fear, is liable to suggest the patient is exaggerating her symptoms. My eyes were opened many years ago when I called to see a farmer's wife and found her in a state of acute anxiety. She was at the height of the attack, her family were helpless and frightened and even I was worried. The patient was pale and sweating. She sat rigidly gripping the arms of her chair and could hardly speak. Her pulse was racing and she looked a very sick woman, but after a short time the symptoms began to moderate. The patient then confided to me that she had often had such attacks, and when they happened she thought she was dying. I could well understand this feeling. Few people who have not experienced a severe emotional upset can appreciate how dreadful the patient can feel, and to attempt to shake them out of the mood with a cheerful slap on the back, real or metaphorical, just does not help. It is very important for depressed and anxious people not to be silenced or made ashamed of their symptoms.

Sometimes the patient knows why she feels so jumpy and ill. She may have a good reason for being worried, that her child is very ill in hospital, for example, but at least she can talk about that to friends. On the other hand she may have cause to doubt her husband's fidelity, but this is a fear she cannot disclose to anyone. If her worries drive her to do something positive, this may help her, but if nothing can be done her anxiety increases.

Anxiety is often made a great deal worse by an alternation of hope and fear. During the war it was recognized that in some ways war widows were better off than the women whose husbands were posted as missing. With the latter, hope gives way to despair and this swing of opposite moods can be very painful, especially as troughs of despair get deeper, and the waves of hope fade away. The whole situation is made worse by the knowledge that the unhappy woman can do nothing positive to help the situation. This feeling of impotence is a great burden.

Sometimes the cause of the worry or the depression is completely hidden from the patient. The anxiety then gives rise to the physical symptoms of fear which have already been described, and the patient thinks she is physically ill, has a bad heart, is developing a cancer or some horrible disease too dreadful to talk about. The more she broods over her feelings the worse they are likely to get.

Life is full of difficulties and worries and it is obvious that we have to work through most of our everyday problems ourselves. Each time we are able to solve such a dilemma our morale is raised and we are better able to cope. If every problem had to be discussed with a social worker, the doctor or the parson, the various services would be completely overwhelmed by trivia and people would become less and less able to overcome difficulties themselves. How then is the patient to decide whether or not to seek advice? If she is married, the problem should be discussed with her husband. This may well ease the situation. If, however, relief is not found then advice should be sought.

If the source of the anxiety is physical illness, or a fear of physical illness, then she should see a doctor as soon as possible. People often worry over something which is, in fact, normal or well within the physiological norm, and a short interview with a sympathetic doctor can put their minds at rest. Two or three times a year I get what I call the "tongue syndrome." The typical case is that of a young person who has been to a party and drunk or smoked too much. She awakens with a mouth which "tastes like the bottom of a parrot's cage." She brushes her teeth well to allay the symptoms and has a good look at her tongue in the mirror. To her horror she sees on the back of the organ a whole set of warty growths which she is quite sure were not there before. She at once concludes she must have a tongue cancer and is in a state of near panic about it. She is so frightened she does not tell a soul about what she thinks, but she may well visit her doctor. She is unlikely to say, "Doctor, I think I have a cancer on the back of my tongue." She is much more likely to complain of a sore throat or a bad taste in her mouth which has made her feel run down. Her mouth looks normal, but one can sense the patient is very worried. Faced with such a case I suggest to the patient she should have a look at my tongue, and I watch for a sense of relief in her eyes as she says, "You have them too." The "warts" are of course normal tastebuds, but many people have not examined their tongues far enough back to realize there are such things. Blemishes in the region of the sexual organs are often a source of anxiety. Small normal sebaceous glands on the penis can worry the male, and innocent tags in the anal or vulval area may frighten the female. One young woman came to see me on the advice of a health visitor, because her husband had discovered she had a lump "down below." The vulva was completely normal, the lump he had discovered was a perfectly normal neck of the womb!

Such simple things as these are often a cause of anxiety which can be completely allayed by a very short examination and talk with the patient, who usually apologizes for having come along with such a silly and trivial complaint. I always reply to this that nothing which causes worry is really trivial. The smallest speck of dust in the eye can cause a great deal of pain and trouble, but one does not argue it is too small to need treatment. Finally, I tell the patient that I would far rather see a hundred such problems to which I can give rapid reassurance, than to see a single neglected case where I feel at once, "Why in heaven's name didn't this patient come along sooner." I advise the patient that it is most important to report all lumps or abnormalities. So many of these are harmless, but the doctor must be allowed to decide about them to ensure nothing that is serious is missed.

The patient who is suffering from anxiety but has no useful knob or rash to show her doctor is in a rather different situation. I tell my patients that, if worry or depression lasts for two weeks, then it is time to see someone about it. It may be easier to talk to the district nurse or a health visitor. If the social worker is not satisfied then she will advise the patient to see her doctor, or she may go and see him direct.

A married woman, thirty years old, with four children came to see me because she was getting so irritable with the family. She found it difficult to sleep at night and she was always exhausted. She was medically examined and there was no physical cause for her trouble. She assured me she had nothing to worry about, so one had to assume that it was possible that something had triggered off anxiety about her health and that after reassurance she would settle down. She was, therefore, given some vitamin tablets and asked to report back in a week's time.

As frequently happens, on her second visit she told me the real cause of her trouble, something she had not liked to mention at her first visit. Her husband was too friendly with a young woman colleague. She had had it out with him since her last visit, and while he had assured her there was nothing in it, and had promised not to see the woman again, she remained unhappy and hurt. She had reared him a fine family and had been a good wife to him and now felt badly repaid. This provided very adequate explanation for her irritability and sleeplessness and had obviously to be resolved in some way before improvement could be expected. To treat the symptoms would be a useless papering over of large cracks.

I asked if I could see both of them together as I knew and liked her husband. The man admitted he had been indiscreet, but it was now all over. I suggested to the wife that we all do silly things from time to time and while she could not forget what had happened, she had to accept it and let bygones be bygones. The following week she saw me again and was much better. She told me that she had continued to brood until she had decided she must do something about it. She went to the works and confronted the other woman. She was rather pleased to find her a plain girl and not the glamorous popsy she had expected. She told the girl what she thought of her and enjoyed her obvious embarrassment, and came away feeling a lot better. The wisdom of this step could, of course, be argued but the patient had a right to tackle her problem in her own way.

Looking at this case history various stages can be distinguished. The woman's marriage was in trouble, she had to turn to someone and she came to her doctor, feeling justified in doing so because her health was being impaired by her anxieties. Initially, she deliberately concealed her problem, but after a thorough examination and reassurance she had been forced to face up to the fact that worry was, in fact, the cause of her troubles. She developed enough courage to confront her husband and to reveal her true feelings to her doctor at her second appointment. Airing the problem and discussing it helped but she did not improve until she helped herself by doing something positive about it. Doctors should always be prepared to listen, sympathize and support while the patient works out a solution to her problems once physical illness has been excluded, but they ought not to give advice outside their specialized sphere. No one could possibly have advised this woman to confront her rival but in her case it worked.

Another rather amusing "do-it-yourself cure" which no social worker could ever advocate occurred many years ago. The woman had eight children, and her husband was the prop at the local working men's club. Every night he was at the club and he worked there continuously at the weekends, while his wife had to run the home and care for the children. She was virtually tied to the kitchen sink with no break in the monotony of life. One day when the man returned home he found eight crying children in the house, and no wife. She had gone back to mother who lived a hundred miles away, having made careful arrangements with the neighbours, who were all sympathetic but completely unhelpful to him. For two days he tried to cope and then gave in. His neighbours readily agreed to look after the children while he went to find his wife. She laid down her terms which he had to accept and they both lived happily ever afterwards! This bold, dangerous move on the part of a frustrated wife succeeded, but no one could ever advise a patient to take such a risk. Such ideas must come from the patient herself. It almost always helps worried patients to do something positive about their problems.

Some patients who have plucked up courage to visit their family doctor may feel disappointed when the doctor has tried to reassure them and told them he can find no evidence of organic disease. The patient should make an effort to accept this opinion, and may well come to realize that in her agitation she had been taking too serious a view of things. The human body is a remarkable and complex machine, and strange and alarming symptoms can develop which have little or no significance. Everyone has the occasional headache, attack of indigestion or twinges of rheumatism. When anxious or depressed these symptoms loom much larger than they should do and may well last longer. A doctor is not involved in the anxieties and can assess the symptoms more objectively, so that his opinion is likely to be correct even if it does not immediately appeal to the patient. If, however, the patient still feels worried and upset after a week or two she should see him again. It may be that she will find the second interview more helpful but if she still feels dissatisfied she should ask for the opinion of a specialist. Where the doctor is quite sure there is no physical basis for the symptoms this may well mean seeing a psychiatrist. People tend to be a bit afraid of this consultant, because the implication is that he deals in mental illness, and "mad people." He does indeed look after people who are seriously disordered but most of his patients are, in fact, just emotionally upset. He is an expert in putting the patient at her ease, and is likely to understand just how she feels. While working in a mental hospital I realized that people arrived feeling tense and fearful, but they quickly discovered that the doctor they were seeing was an ordinary, understanding kind of fellow, and that talking to such a person could make them feel better at once.

Before seeing any such doctor it is necessary for the patient to have a clear idea of what results can reasonably be hoped for. If she consults a doctor about an insoluble problem it is unreasonable to expect some magical remedy. The doctor has no wand to raise the dead, or to bring back a wayward husband who has gone off with another woman. Talking to a sympathetic listener helps in many ways. If you hold a newspaper an inch from your nose, you will not be able to read a word, but if held a foot or so away the type comes into focus, and can be read. In the same way we are often too close to our problems and we tend to misinterpret them. Talking to a skilled listener helps to get things into perspective, and it may even help to develop ideas to how to tackle a life situation more adequately. The advisor, whoever he or she is, will not give direct advice about central problems, but the patient may, nonetheless, receive useful guidance that will put her in a better position to fight her own battle.

It is, for instance, important to have regular meals, however poor the appetite. It may seem easier to skip the odd meal but it is wrong to do so. If alcohol is taken regularly a careful watch must be kept that the usual ration is not exceeded. It may be tempting to use it as a kind of tranquillizer if an extra glass of beer or sherry is found to improve the mood, but it is dangerous to rely upon it too much in a period of stress as this may lead to addiction. Simple things like fresh air and exercise are beneficial in this kind of sickness as in health. Activity in the home or in the garden, or a walk in the park or countryside, help far more than sitting about moping; while doing things for other people is a very good antidote for self-pity.

Few problems are helped by dwelling on them in solitude and turning them over and over in the mind, just as it does not really help a plant to keep pulling it up to see how the roots are growing. Hopes and fears should be discussed freely with a spouse, but not constantly or even the most patient listener will grow weary. It is a mistake to tell all one's troubles to friends for they are unlikely to be able to give constructive help. If they are too sympathetic they increase self-pity; if they are hard or uninterested they inflict pain. Going over troubles just brings them again uncomfortably to the forefront of the mind, and should be avoided unless it is going to serve some useful purpose.

A depressed or anxious person cannot change her feelings by thinking about things nor by willing herself to be better, but she can adhere to a healthy programme and follow the practical advice she is given. The sad person cannot make herself cheerful, but she can, with an effort, eat regular meals and occupy herself with simple jobs about the house. Exhaustion may call for rest, but this must be regulated and not allowed to degenerate into lying about in a heap for most of the day.

DRUG TREATMENT

Many patients who visit the doctor expect to get some tablets or medicine to help their symptoms. The treatment of emotional illnesses by such methods will be dealt with later in greater detail, but some things need to be said at this point. Drugs for depression, especially if it is an endogenous type of depression, can be very useful, but drugs to allay anxiety tend to create more problems than they cure. It should be remembered that, in the first place, anxiety is a useful reaction, a protective mechanism. It may be uncomfortable to be keyed up before an important interview or examination or over some crisis in life but if the tension leads to swifter action or drives one to think out some solution it is obviously a mistake to seek to be relieved of this anxiety. Even where the tension and anxiety serve no useful purpose its treatment should be approached with much caution.

Drugs which rapidly allay the butterflies in the stomach and relax the patient in a matter of a quarter of an hour easily become drugs of addiction. They are such a comfort that the patient soon finds she cannot live without them and, in the case of the fast acting barbiturates like sodium amytal, they may well be taken in ever larger doses so that the patient can end up in a state of chronic intoxication with slurred speech and a reeling gait like an alcoholic. These drugs augment or facilitate the action of alcohol and, if both are taken together, it can be very dangerous. Slow acting barbiturates like phenobarbitone do not give the sudden relaxation or "kicks" of sodium amytal, are therefore less dangerous, and are not so popular.

Soon after the antidepressant drugs were introduced a number of new tranquillizers called Librium, Valium and Serenid D were produced, and these were said to have the same effect on anxiety as the antidepressive group had on depression. They certainly relieved the tension in anxiety and were less dangerous than the quick acting barbiturates, but still, if taken for any length of time, the patient finds it very hard to do without them. The majority of patients who find comfort in their Librium capsules are reluctant to stop taking them even when the crisis which caused the anxiety has passed. It is much easier for the doctor to write out a prescription for a hundred tablets than to sit and listen to the patient's problem and to help her to solve it or to live with it, but the latter course is better medicine. Some patients who have spent a whole hour with a psychiatrist come away disgruntled because they "did not get any treatment." They have not realized the importance of airing their problems to an expert ear. To some extent the psychiatrist is at fault if the patient leaves him dissatisfied because, with any treatment, time should be taken to explain to the patient what is happening and what the doctor intends to do. After such an interview I always make a point of saying to the patient, "If I had given you a bottle of medicine I could have got rid of you a quarter of an hour ago, but I feel it is far more important to discuss your problems and the possible causes of your distress."

SLEEP AND SLEEPLESSNESS

Our grandparents used to worry about constipation. The bowels had to be moved every day after breakfast, and if this did not happen they became very worried because "bowel intoxication" could cause a lot of trouble. So they dosed themselves with Epsom salts or castor oil, or even inserted an irritating "soap pill" into the rectum. People today seem to be just as worried about the importance of sleep. If the patient does not get a good night's sleep she panics and rushes to the doctor for sleeping tablets.

Parish[1] showed that in the six years 1965–70 some forty-three per cent of all drugs given for nervous disorders were sleeping tablets. In all the Western countries more and more hypnotics are consumed every year. Between 1954 and 1959 the sales of barbiturates doubled. These figures had levelled off in the early sixties but in 1965 new hypnotics were launched which were advertised as being non-barbiturate, safe, and producing natural sleep. The sales of these drugs soared, and while some fall occurred in the sale of barbitures, the overall total of sleeping tablets rose once more. It has been estimated that some ten per cent of all prescriptions in Britain are for sleeping tablets.

We spend almost a third of our lives asleep and until recently surprisingly little was known about what happened to the brain during that time. This organ is a complex miniaturized computer made up of millions of tiny cells, all of which have an electric component. As long ago as 1924 Hans Berger, a German psychiatrist, first recorded the cerebral electrical potentials of the human brain, and this was the beginning of a new and valuable medical instrument called the electroencephalogram (E.E.G.). Used on volunteers to investigate sleep, it has revealed that there are various levels including a deep dreamless state, and a lighter form of sleep in which rapid eye movements (R.E.M.) occur. It is during this latter period that the subject is dreaming.

It has been found that the average normal sleep consists of

[1] Parish, P. (1971). *Journal of the Royal College of General Practitioners*, Suppl. 4, **21**, 92.

a deep trough lasting about one and a half hours followed by about twenty minutes of R.E.M. sleep and then another trough. R.E.M. sleep occurs on average four or five times each night.

It seems that R.E.M. sleep serves a very useful purpose and that dreams are necessary for refreshing sleep. Some people will say they never dream, but all normal people do have R.E.M. episodes of sleep and, if awakened when this eye movement is indicated on the E.E.G. recording, even the so-called non-dreamers will admit to dreams which they then rapidly forget. If sleeping tablets are taken the amount of R.E.M. sleep is drastically reduced, and from this one can infer that such artificial sleep is less refreshing than normal sleep. If the drugs are withdrawn there is an immediate increase in the amount of R.E.M. sleep, the patient dreams excessively and may well have nightmares. When drugs are withdrawn from people who are really addicted to them the rebound of R.E.M. sleep is especially large and can be very unpleasant. In alcoholics such R.E.M. sleep accounts for all of the sleeping time, and then the terrifying state of delirium tremens can occur.

Not only do sleeping tablets produce only a second rate form of sleep but also, like tranquillizers, they are very habit forming and the more rapid the action the greater the danger of habituation. It is very pleasant to go to bed and "go out like a light," but in time the drug tends to lose its effect and the dose is increased until the patient is intoxicated with it. If the hypnotic is slow acting, there is no pleasant rapid onset of sleep, and the drug, which is only slowly excreted, carries over into the next day. The patient may well have a kind of hangover, and research has shown that work efficiency the next day is likely to be diminished.

I was once admitted to hospital for a few weeks and, to ensure that I slept well and was a good patient at night, I was given sleeping pills and I much enjoyed the experience. I continued to take them when I got home until I realized that it was a bad habit which did not really help the brain to recharge its batteries, as it were, in a normal physiological way. I decided to stop the tablets and I soon discovered how hard it is to give them up. I dreaded going to bed, as I knew I would not go off to sleep for a very long time. I used to toss and turn in a state of acute anxiety wondering how I could ever do my work the next day, always supposing I survived to see the dawn! Then I would remember that if only I stretched out my hand to find the sleeping pills, relaxation and sleep would rapidly supervene, and this temptation had to be resisted. The whole process of weaning myself from the habit was almost as difficult as giving up smoking, and it took about six weeks to get over the nightly recurrent sleep crises. I am not a good sleeper now, but to lie awake or to awaken early does not worry me at all. The anguish I have tried to describe has completely gone and I awaken far more refreshed. I never feel I cannot face the day's work after a bad night.

Sleep is necessary, but most people can do with far less sleep than they imagine they need. Hospital nurses often remark that the patient who claims not to have slept a wink was snoring on and off all night. Electroencephalogram recordings have confirmed that this is indeed what happens. Under experimental conditions volunteers who claimed not to have slept were shown to have had the typical sleep rhythms on the E.E.G. tracings during most of the night. It has to be accepted that it is quite impossible to know how much sleep one has had during a "sleepless night" and that usually it proves to be quite enough. The thing that often makes wakefulness distressing is that in the darkness and quiet, morbid thoughts are frequently allowed to fill the mind, and it is these thoughts and not the lack of rest that cause the weariness next day. I was much impressed some years ago by a very wise and charming widow who told me she found sleeplessness the most distressing feature when she lost her husband until she decided that if she had to be awake she would make good use of the time by going over all the lovely holidays they had had and all their happiest times together and lack of sleep ceased to bother her from then on.

Having said all this about tranquillizing drugs and sleeping tablets, I feel there is a place for them *in an emergency*, but any course should be limited to a week or so, and the patient should be warned of this in advance. A week or so of sleeping tablets does not appear to have the bad effect on sleep described above, and no serious habituation is likely to arise in that time. One winter I was called out because two small children had fallen through some ice and been drowned, and you can imagine the mental state of the unhappy parents. They were given a very heavy dose of drugs to take at night to black out their misery. I told them what I was going to do, and I promised to give such help for a few nights. After a week they were prepared to do without such drugs, and have never had them since. The same could be said of tranquillizers. They are useful in a crisis, but only for a very limited time, and the patient must be warned of this from the onset.

In the past, before I realized the dangers of this type of drug, I prescribed them as freely as any doctor, so there are in the practice many patients more or less permanently on hypnotics and sedatives. The majority will come to no harm, only a very few may find themselves taking bigger and bigger doses to get the desired effect. I have one old woman of ninety who has had her nembutal at night for twenty years. She has never increased the dose, and the drug appears to have no ill effect. Winston Churchill according to Lord Moran[2] had sleeping tablets every night during the war, and this did not appear to diminish either his drive or his mental capacity, so readers who are taking these drugs regularly without requiring increased doses need not be alarmed. What I have tried to emphasize is that these drugs are not a simple answer to anxiety or sleeplessness and today I personally very rarely use them except in short courses. Those who are permanently on tranquillizers by day may be able to cut down the dose by taking the tablets only when they need them, when, in fact, they are face to face with a particularly stressful situation. It is sensible to take aspirins to ease the pain when one has a headache, but it would be foolish to take them regularly three times a day in case a headache developed.

Drugs to combat depression are quite a different kettle of fish from the hypnotic and sedative group I have just described.

[2] Lord Moran, *Winston Churchill* (Constable, 1966).

These drugs are indeed potent medicines and they need to be taken regularly, often in large doses, for quite a long time. As a general rule I prescribe them for three months in persons under thirty years of age and for six months for those over the age of thirty. This is of course just a useful rule of thumb to guide doctors, or to answer the patient's question, "Will I always have to take these tablets?" They are usually quite easy to drop as so often they have inconvenient side effects. Some of them cause a very dry mouth, giddiness when the patient stands up, visual difficulties, and all sorts of queer feelings. With another group of drugs all sorts of food items are restricted such as cheese, broad beans and alcohol. The patient is only too pleased to give up the drugs when he is better to get rid of the dry mouth, and to be allowed a full and normal diet.

Patients' reactions to drugs vary enormously. It is imperative that patients on these drugs should try to take them exactly as prescribed. They do no good in the bottle! The "side effects" may be trying at first but usually pass off and should be tolerated if possible. However, if this proves too difficult and the patient feels she cannot continue to take them, she must get in touch with her doctor and discuss the matter with him. He may be able to help by adjusting the dose or changing the tablets. It is folly to stop them and do nothing until the next appointment. The sooner the maximum dose is reached, the sooner the wretched symptoms of depression will stop, so it is well worth persevering. Antidepressant tablets often take two or even three weeks before they are effective. There are no rapid results with these drugs, which is another good reason for them not becoming drugs of addiction.

RECURRENT ATTACKS

Between a fifth and a quarter of depressed patients have only one attack, the majority have recurrent episodes, and a few unhappy people have two or three attacks every year. Fortunately with modern treatment such attacks can be aborted or brought under control pretty quickly. It is most important for patients to accept treatment as soon as they or the next of kin are certain a relapse is on the way.

There is very often a sense of shame left when a depressive episode has passed. The patient tends to make light of what has happened, and tries to forget the whole horrid affair. When a recurrent attack looms, far more often than not she tries to cover up and keeps saying to herself that this time she is going to master it on her own. Even after several attacks over which the patient has been helped by a sympathetic doctor, she still hates the idea of confessing to a relapse. We all have our bad days and, while the depressed patient should not be encouraged to seek help for every minor lapse, if the mood persists for a couple of weeks it is time to see the doctor.

Some patients come to recognize warning symptoms. One woman knew when her dentures became uncomfortable and she started fiddling with her teeth that a new episode of depression was imminent. A man who had a regular pint of beer at the local every night, recognized he was slipping when he had insufficient energy to go out after a day's work.

I really feel I have won the confidence of the patient who will come along to see me after such a short preliminary period of depression, but such patients are a minority. Because of this it is really advisable to persuade the spouse or someone who is close to the patient to act as a link. Some of these relatives are very quick to see the red light and urge the patient to consult a doctor. When I started to work on this problem almost thirty years ago there was no remedy and no easy answer to a very unpleasant illness. I could ensure a good night's rest by giving hypnotics, and the only drug which had any effect on depression was amphetamine or the "purple heart" type of tablet. The good effect was only marginal, and they were soon found to be highly addictive so are rarely used today. Then, one's main function was to reassure, and keep on reassuring the depressed patient that the mood would pass, but after weeks or months of misery any words of consolation rang a bit hollow to both doctor and patient, but there was nothing else one could do for the so-called mild depression. Electroconvulsive treatment was available only in a mental hospital for those who were ill enough or brave enough to seek admission.

Today all this has changed and the family doctor who is experienced in this kind of work can help the vast numbers of depressed patients who come his way to recovery in quite a short space of time. Drug treatment is often the keystone to success in such cases.

4

The Role of Relatives

DEPRESSION

Mental illness is still a weird and very frightening business, and anyone who is suddenly confronted with an acute mental breakdown in a relative is quite naturally distressed. If an ageing parent has a stroke, or is laid low by a coronary thrombosis, this is upsetting enough, but the parent is still the parent. The family can talk to him, and sympathize with him, discuss family affairs perhaps, and in general retain a relationship with him. If, on the other hand, he suddenly becomes abjectly depressed, that relationship is lost. Not only is the parent very ill, but he is not approachable in a rational way. A previously sensible and normal person keeps talking about the sins of his youth, how he had once had venereal disease and is now paying for all his misdeeds, how he is damned for eternity and everyone in the village knows about it, and will someone get him a shot gun so that he can expiate his sins and end his misery. Similarly many aged parents who suffer from what used to be called a second childhood, can cause great distress to the family. The revered old mother may become a complete cabbage, unable to remember a thing or contribute anything to the life of the family, a complete caricature of her former self. She may smile sweetly when approached by her son, but she has no idea who he is. She has no knowledge of where she lives, or what is happening, and she may well become wet and dirty. It can really be said that the beloved and respected personality has died and only the pathetic shrunken shell survives.

It is even more alarming when acute mental illness occurs in younger people, and husbands and wives, or sons and daughters begin to behave irrationally and cannot be "reached" by their anxious relatives. Fortunately a sudden acute mental breakdown, horrifying and distressing though it may be, usually carries with it the promise of recovery, and this thought should be a great consolation to the relatives. Simple drug treatment may help many of them very rapidly and even very old people sometimes respond well to electro convulsive therapy, which is really a safe treatment.

The depressed old man described earlier can lose all his symptoms on a course of drugs, or he may need E.C.T. to expedite his recovery. A retired couple of seventy lived in the practice area, and the old woman suddenly became very agitated and ill. She was sure that she had some incurable disease and that she was too ill to be helped. She could not sleep or eat and wandered around the house all day weeping and moaning, "Oh dear, oh dear." She did not respond to drugs, and a psychiatrist was asked to call and see her. He confirmed that she had an agitated depression, and she was so ill that he felt any treatment with E.C.T. would have to take place in hospital. As she already had a brother and a sister as permanent residents in the local psychiatric hospital, she did not like the idea. She assured her husband and me that she would never leave the hospital alive, and the husband was very upset and pessimistic. However, six weeks later she returned home an entirely different person, rational, smiling and able to cope.

The same kind of thing can happen with young people. A schizophrenic episode can appear quite suddenly, and the normal youngster of yesterday becomes a strange, haunted creature.

One Saturday morning a young woman called to see me because she had found people were talking about her. At the office they had said she was pregnant, and she heard voices which accused her of various things. She looked wild eyed and agitated, and it was very difficult to follow what she had to say. She left me to go to the police station to complain of her persecutors. I saw her parents later the same morning and they were beside themselves with worry. She had been behaving strangely for only two or three days and, fortunately, agreed to be treated by me. She was given large doses of the appropriate drugs and slept for five days, waking only for food or to go to the lavatory. The dosage was then reduced so that when she saw a psychiatrist she would be able to talk to him. When the consultant saw her nine days after my initial interview he could find no evidence of any mental abnormality. With prompt and adequate treatment the mental illness, which had looked very sinister to me, melted away. This was ten years ago. She is now married with a family and there has been no recurrence of her illness.

Sudden depressive reactions are not uncommon in young people, but here the victim appears inexplicably anxious or depressed, without the bizarre symptoms of schizophrenia. A mother brought her nineteen year old daughter to see me. The young woman was in great distress, unable to sleep, and was very upset about her impending marriage. She wanted to hand the ring back and call the whole thing off. As she gave no logical reason for this her boy friend was certain she was ill. She had that intense anxiety which is so typical of depression. She was persuaded that she must have a course of treatment and if, when she felt better, she still wanted to break off her engagement she should be free to do so, but to wait a few weeks before making up her mind. She responded rapidly to treatment. The marriage took place and she has now been married for twelve years. Important decisions must never be taken when a person is depressed. Both the family and the family doctor should persuade the patient to wait until the depressive mood has passed. This girl's romance might well have been blighted had she been allowed to act on impulse.

In dealing with old people the problems are often less easily resolved. Unfortunately the patient suffering from senile dementia will not respond to any treatment available today as this is an incurable degenerative disease of the brain. When faced with such a case, however, it is worth considering the possibility of a masked or coexisting depression even in these old folk. Treatment may produce a remarkable recovery since the symptoms may be due, at least in part, to a treatable depression rather than an untreatable dementia. Without it the patient usually deteriorates, although some manage to live through the depression and make an unexpected recovery.

Many years ago an elderly brother and sister lived in the village. The old woman died and the man became more and more helpless. The house was neglected, he did not feed himself and was quite unable to cope. He appeared a typical case of senile dementia and he was admitted to the geriatric ward in the local psychiatric hospital, after which I lost sight of him. In 1969, when I was doing a long-term follow-up of all psychiatric hospital admissions[1], I traced him to an old people's home in another village, and there I found him a spritely old man of eighty-five in full possession of his faculties. The diagnosis of dementia had been wrong. He had become depressed after the loss of his sister and the depression had ultimately cleared, leaving him mentally completely normal. If I had been able to treat him with drugs in the first place, he might well have recovered in the community, and his hospital admission would have been unnecessary. Now that drugs are available treatment should be given if there is any possibility of depression. This treatment will do no harm if the patient is in fact demented, but if depression is the basic trouble it could produce a dramatic improvement.

No one could fail to observe the onset of a sudden mental illness such as I have just described, but many breakdowns have an insidious onset, and it is often quite impossible to say just when the illness started. In cases like this it is much more difficult for relatives to seek help. The husband may realize that his wife is less and less able to cope with her work, the house is becoming untidy, the food badly prepared and normal sex life a thing of the past, but when he mentions any of these things she flies off the handle and declares that he is imagining things. If he suggests she should see a doctor she will make any excuse to evade this issue and avoid a medical consultation. In such circumstances it is quite justifiable for the husband to seek a consultation with the doctor to discuss the problem. If the wife

[1] Watts, C. A. H. (1970). *Journal of the Royal College of General Practitioners*, **20**, 79.

refuses to visit the doctor, the doctor may decide to call and see her at home, but the husband must then tell the wife what he has done to prepare the ground for a useful consultation. It is quite useless to ask a doctor just to drop in as if it was a friendly visit. The patient must know in advance it is a medical consultation and not just a social occasion. Sick people must not be subjected to trickery even in a good cause. At the same time discretion can be used. If the wife is likely to make a scene, or even do a disappearing act, she need not be told until the very last moment, but it is unfair to both the patient and the doctor to meet on false terms. Deception can so damage the relationship as to make a useful consultaion almost impossible.

RECURRENT ILLNESS

Here again the next of kin have a very important part to play. Many depressed patients, for instance, are subject to recurrent bouts of depression. It has already been suggested that a number of these patients are most reluctant to see a doctor about their troubles, even when they will admit he has helped them in the past. As the old saying goes, "a spectator sees more of the game than a player," and a husband can often detect a recurrent episode of depression before his wife is fully aware of what is happening. Because of this I usually make a point of advising the next of kin to take the initiative if he or she feels the patient is relapsing into illness. They are often very quick at spotting significant symptoms. The sleep may become restless, the eye lacking in its usual lustre, the wife may become very irritable, or there is a tell tale falling off of domestic efficiency. If such a mood lasts for two weeks, it is time advice was sought. If it is a false alarm, there is no harm done, but it is quite wrong to leave such a patient in misery for several weeks before taking steps to help her, even if she continues to insist that she does not need help. Many women who will not see a doctor on their own will go to the surgery if the husband is prepared to go too. They are often grateful for such action even though they protest all the way to the surgery that it is just a waste of the doctor's time.

There are some other situations in which the illness of the patient is such that medical intervention has to be initiated by the next of kin.

MANIA

Mania is the opposite of depression. The patient feels elated, becomes very talkative and can be both witty and amusing. The cheerful vigour of the patient is infectious and the observer may be quite impressed and enter into her mood of exhilaration. The manic person is very active and can work day and night, she seems to need very little sleep. Mild episodes of this are called hypomania, and they do no harm but, if severe, mania is a very distressing condition for all but the patient, who usually thoroughly enjoys her state of elation. People who have experienced mania say that anyone who has never had such excitement has never really lived. Feeling like this, full of drive and confidence, it is not surprising that the patient is unwilling to consult a doctor; why, indeed should she when she has never felt better in her life. She is, however, very difficult to live with. She talks constantly, often spends her money far too freely, drinks too heavily, wears her poor husband out with her excessive sexual demands, and may well commit rather stupid sexual indiscretions. She never wants to sleep. She has irresponsible impulses, wants to adopt several children, buy a new house, do a world tour; and, if the husband tries to argue he cannot afford such luxuries, his objections are brushed aside. Fortunately the powers of concentration are poor, and before she has finalized the world cruise at the travel agency, she may have some other idea to pursue. If crossed in any way the manic patient can become very angry or even violent, but the mood soon passes and the exuberant jollity soon returns. Depression in a relative is an unpleasant condition to endure, but mania can be a far worse experience.

Fortunately today, mania like depression is a treatable illness.

56

If the condition is mild no harm is done. One woman described her feelings as follows: "Never for years had I felt so energetic. In fact I simply could not sit down for two minutes at a time. I worked like fury in the house, and did all manner of jobs in the greenhouse and in the garden. I often started to bake and do other jobs at 8.oo p.m. I picked pounds of fruit in the garden from which I made 90 lbs of jam, all done in an evening when normally I would have been reading or relaxing in some way. I have been completely happy working for fourteen to fifteen hours a day. My husband tried to make me rest more, but I told him it is like telling someone with measles to wipe off the rash. I could not sit still long enough to talk to callers." She realized she was "too high" and was prepared to accept treatment: but this was exceptional. Unfortunately most manic patients are quite unprepared to see a doctor or have any treatment.

The wife of a man who used to swing from one extreme to the other described their family life as follows. "When he is depressed he says very little. He goes out to work, but I realize it is an effort for him. He cannot sleep at night and, of course, he keeps me awake. I get worried if he is late home wondering if anything awful has happened. If I ask him to see the doctor, he snaps my head off. Social life grinds to a halt. We never go out together, we never entertain. Then the mood changes and he demands parties, but these are most embarrassing as no one does any talking except my husband. Something has to happen every night. If we go to a dance he carries on until I am exhausted. If we go to a show, he may well walk out in the middle complaining loudly it's a lousy performance, and I follow him feeling thoroughly uncomfortable and ashamed. He buys a new car, a new refrigerator and is obviously spending far more than we can afford. I hate to see him depressed, but I dread the manic episodes far, far more." Effective treatment of a severe case like this would only be possible in a hospital. However, such cases are very rare. Over the years I have treated well over two thousand cases of depression and a few with elation, but only four have had to go to hospital because of severe mania. Some six per cent of all patients with depression experience a period of elation.

Depression: The Blue Plague

The mildest cases need no treatment and the remainder can be controlled by drug therapy. Blood tests may be necessary, but adequate treatment can usually be established without any great inconvenience to the patient.

THE PARANOID PERSONALITY

Some people are suspicious or jealous by nature and if they become depressed they may well develop a persecution complex. This type of problem is best illustrated by a case history.

A woman aged forty-five had lost her husband after a long and painful illness. She was very upset by his death and became obsessed with the idea she had contracted his disease. She was seen by the appropriate specialist and received reassurance, but she remained unconvinced and a very unhappy woman. She was a great problem to her children who were most concerned about her. This occurred before the days of drug treatment for depression. When advised to see a psychiatrist, she became very indignant : she wasn't mad, she knew perfectly well what was wrong with her and this was just an attempt to get rid of her. It was a very unhappy situation. She left her daughter and went to live in a small terrace house, and here it was that her paranoid, persecutory ideas developed. She was sure that her neighbours were listening at her walls, or even climbing across the false floor to pry on her, and that passing cars which hooted or flashed their lights did so to annoy her. Once again I was called in to see her. She was very suspicious but knew me well and agreed reluctantly to be treated by me. By this time new drugs were available, and these fortunately did the trick. She lost her depression, ceased to complain of her neighbours and everyone was delighted with her progress.

This was an unusually happy solution, for such suspicious people are often very difficult to treat. They may well refuse to see a doctor altogether or, having been persuaded to see him, may refuse to take the treatment he advises. If a psychiatrist is suggested they at once conclude that a plot is being hatched against them. A woman will imply that her husband wants her

58

locked up in hospital so that he can live his double life with his fancy woman unmolested. Treatment can usually help such people, but the problem is often to get them to accept help from a doctor or a specialist, and as with the manic patient, it is the next of kin who have to take the initiative and get the doctor to see the patient. Any consultation requires the greatest tact and patience.

The Chronic Patient

So far I have confined my attention to patients who respond to treatment. Unfortunately in the present state of knowledge, there are still some depressed people who do not respond to any form of treatment, who remain unhappy, miserable people for years on end. Such a patient can have accepted willingly every form of treatment offered, all kinds of drugs, hours of psychotherapy, hospital treatment with E.C.T. and all the latest ideas, but nothing seems to do them any good. It is not surprising if the relatives of such people form the opinion that modern psychiatry is useless, for in their long and very painful experience it has been so and they have no opportunity to meet the vastly greater number of people who have been helped to recovery.

Chronic depressives can be divided into two types. With some patients the depression is a continuous painful process from which there appears to be no relief. With another type of person the patient literally "enjoys poor health " and her depression is used to manipulate circumstances, often appearing to give her a good deal of subtle satisfaction. These two forms of depression will be considered in more detail.

The chronic painful depression is illustrated by the woman who loses her husband and the process of mourning is carried on for several years. She feels as wretched and bereaved ten years after his death as on the day he died. She can have every form of psychiatric treatment available, in hospital or at home, but nothing really helps her. She enjoys the oblivion of sleep and tends to become habituated to heavy doses of sleeping tablets. She lives a sad, lonely and wretched life. The following case history illustrates another type of painful chronic depression in greater detail.

The patient was the second child in a family of four, and at the age of seventeen fell out with the family and found lodgings. It was not long before her landlady began to complain about her and asked her to find new rooms. She had a young man so she married him and together they found furnished accommodation, but still nothing was right and they had to move on again. At last they found a small cottage in our village, and she came to see me. She was an unhappy young woman who seemed unable to get on well with people. She blamed herself and her "big mouth," but she felt low, irritable and depressed. There were no particular problems, but there was no joy in life. Her husband was a tolerant, long suffering man, who found it hard to explain her moods. She was a good cook and housekeeper, but she had little interest in sex and never wanted to go out. She saw a psychiatrist who said she suffered from a personality problem and no treatment was suggested. Then she became pregnant and for nine months she was a different woman, calm, happy and contented. There were no more rows with either her family or her neighbours. She had an easy normal birth, but two weeks after the confinement she was far worse than she had ever been. She started to hate her child, and was so distraught she had to be admitted to a psychiatric hospital. She had E.C.T. and after two months returned home, improved but far from well. She derived little joy from her baby and life continued to be a real burden for her. She used to see me regularly, always apologizing for wasting my time. I could never uncover any cause for her misery, and even when antidepressant drugs came along, they did not help her. Gradually she improved, and her visits became less frequent, until they stopped. She was not really well but had learned to accept life as she found it. I once asked her what was the happiest time in her life and without any hesitation she replied, when she was carrying her infant. During pregnancy the blend of hormones had had a quite remarkable effect upon her, followed unfortunately by a complete breakdown after the birth. Nothing I could do by way of drugs or hormone tablets could reproduce the tranquillity of her pregnancy, but this was an experiment she dared not repeat, as the aftermath of her child-birth had been far too devastating. For several years she had remained a very unhappy young woman whose greatest asset was her kindly husband who refused to be broken by her moods and tantrums. When at her worst after the birth, E.C.T. had brought her back to normal : but normality for her was a state of chronic depression.

The second type of chronic depression is one in which the symptoms appear to be used by the patient to manipulate those around her. Many of these patients could be called hypochondriacs. The patient is preoccupied by her health, and even more by symptoms of ill health. The French dramatist Molière gave a brilliant description of such a patient in his play *Le Malade Imaginaire*. The problem of the illness and the difficulties and temptations it created for the medical profession are portrayed in a satirical way. The unhappy patient is ridiculed and the grasping doctors are shown to be no better than charlatans. This was of course written some three hundred years ago. There was no National Health Service in those days !

The hypochondriac is constantly aware of body sensations. She feels her pulse, she examines her tongue in the mirror each morning. She becomes so obsessed with how she feels that she can think of little else. Besides being an illness it is a way of life. Every waking moment has some bearing on her health and life can easily become one long ritual. She may feel frightened and ill at times, but in general her symptoms seem to give some bizarre satisfaction to her. She is the chemists' best friend, and will accept any new remedy offered her by her doctor or her friends and neighbours. She buys proprietary medicines freely, and is a constant visitor to the herbalist. Some of these features are depicted in the following case history.

The woman I have in mind was sixty when I first came across her. She was a widow, but she was looked after by an unmarried son and daughter, who were completely dominated by her. Another daughter had disgraced herself by leaving home and getting married, and was, as a result, very unpopular with the rest of the family, especially the mother. The old woman's medical file was the thickest in the practice, and she was visited on average once a week, but more often when she was ill, and she was very frequently ill. When first seen in any episode of illness she looked very poorly and, as a new doctor to the area, I was alarmed by her symptoms and appearance, but after a while I learned she was an accomplished actress. If she was not visited regularly she would fall ill, terrify the family and send in alarming messages, always out of hours, and I soon found from bitter experience that it was easier for all concerned to call weekly. The daughter had to bear the brunt of the burden and I was very sorry for her. One year, by putting pressure on the family, I persuaded her to go away for a week's holiday. On this occasion her brother was free to help as he also was on holiday and he was prepared to look after his mother assisted by a home help. Two days later I had to visit her in the middle of the night. She had taken ill and made her son get the police to contact her daughter who got a taxi home, found her mother looking ghastly and she was ordered to send for me. Once more I could find no evidence of serious illness, and she lived another eight years before she had a stroke and died.

This old woman really enjoyed her "illness" and with it she dominated her family, and her family doctor. If the attention of either lapsed, she could produce such dramatic symptoms they were soon brought to heel. She refused to see a psychiatrist, and felt insulted by the suggestion. She was, however, prepared to see any number of other specialists and enjoyed investigations as long as they did not cause her too much inconvenience, but an organic basis for her symptoms was never found. Unlike the previous patient who was depressed and unhappy, this woman, despite her appearance, revelled in her illness because with it she could get almost anything she wanted. Three hundred years ago a physician described the hypochondriasis as follows,[2] "It is called the disgrace of physicians because they seldom cure it: it is also called the scourge of physicians as they who have it are continually asking for new medicines and presently wearying

[2] Riverius, L., *The Practice of Physick* (1661).

therewith, and daily complain to the physician and often change them." This was a very good description of my patient except on one count. Unfortunately for me, she never changed her physician. I would have been delighted had she done so.

This type of person will stoop to any deception to attract attention if she feels she is being ignored, and it is patently obvious to everyone but herself that this is her objective. The husband of such a woman once told me that she had attempted to commit suicide. It was a cold March afternoon, and when he returned from work he found his wife up to her neck in water in the water butt. "I feel sure she only did it to impress me," the husband suggested. "I think she waited by the back door until she heard my footsteps in the passage, and then she stepped into the water butt. If I was going to commit suicide," he said, "I should have gone in head first!" On one occasion I found her in bed flushed and sweating. There were beads of perspiration on her forehead, and the bed literally steamed when I threw back the bed clothes to examine her. To my surprise I could find no evidence of serious illness, and her temperature was normal. I was puzzled until her husband followed me to the car. He told me that she had gone back to bed after breakfast with two hot water bottles. She had put on extra blankets and had spent most of the morning covered completely with bed clothes to keep up the sweat. She had emerged from the bed clothes as far as her neck, when she heard me on the stairs!

With patients such as this the doctor has to support and help the relatives who carry the heavy burden of responsibility, not just for a short visit, but all the time, week after week. They are in far more need of help than the patient.

ALCOHOLISM

Another type of patient who refuses to consult a doctor, while at the same time very prone to depression, is the alcoholic addict. Alcoholism is an illness which is not recognized as such by the public at large nor by the medical profession as a whole, and the burden of trying to carry on family life falls heavily on the unaffected partner. It is perfectly proper to consult your family doctor if you have such a patient in the family, but it is not an easy problem to treat as the victim rarely wants to give up his drinking or see a doctor. Any relative who is interested in this problem should consult another book in this series especially written to cover this subject.[3]

RELATIVES IN CRISES

It cannot be repeated too often that any depressive upset which lasts for a fortnight or more should be reported. An acute or severe disturbance should be dealt with even sooner. It is surprising how clever relatives can be at realizing that the patient is a suicidal risk. If after a consultation I find the patient has suicidal ideas, I make a point of telling the next of kin. They are rarely surprised and usually say that because of this the patient has never been left alone. There is a common saying which suggests that if a person threatens to commit suicide, she will never do it. This is nonsense. Any threat of suicide should be taken seriously and medical advice sought at once. Relatives do, in fact, frequently take lifesaving action in this way. For instance, I was once treating a young man for what I thought was an anxiety state about his heart. His wife rang me up to say she was extremely worried about him. She had been a secretary to a business man who had killed himself and she felt sure her husband had the same kind of illness. She brought him along within the hour and I discussed the whole situation with the man. His wife was quite right. He was in fact suffering from a depression, and he improved quickly when given antidepressant drugs. When he was better he told me just how low he had sunk and related his fearful thoughts at that time. "I often felt tempted," he said, "to drive my car full tilt into a tree or the side of a bridge. No one would have suspected suicide." Relatives like his wife are indeed the most important "spotters" in the

[3] Glatt, M. M., *The Alcoholic and the Help He Needs* (Priory Press, 1970).

community. They are, as it were, the first line of defence with this type of illness.

If a patient has a suicidal urge, his life is in danger, and as a rule the general practitioner will seek specialist advice. Many of these patients, for their own protection, need to be treated in hospital. Even in such desperate situations, however, there may be occasions when this is not possible or convenient. One Christmas Eve a farmer was brought along to see me by two angry and rather frightened sons. They had found him fastening a rope with a noose at one end, to a beam in a barn. Christmas Eve is not the easiest time to get a second opinion or an urgent hospital admission. It was decided therefore to keep the man at home until after the holiday. The younger men were advised never to leave their father alone but to be tactful and unobtrusive in their observation of him and he was given full doses of anti-depressant drugs. He was very carefully supervised by his family and, in fact, improved so rapidly that admission to hospital was never necessary. He was visited regularly at home to give close supervision and support to both the patient and relatives.

Fuller consideration of the doctor's role in such situations will be given in the next chapter; here we are concerned with the relations. A close kinsman, especially a husband, can be a great moral support to his wife if he takes her along to see the doctor. He may be able to describe some of her symptoms better than she could, as she may well find it hard to express her feelings in words. It is important that he should know what treatment is suggested, and then at home he can help by seeing that the tablets are taken in the right dose at the right time. He should see that there is no danger of the patient taking an overdose. If side effects worry or upset the patient he can, if need be, seek further advice from the doctor. If he knows what is going on he can with confidence encourage his wife to put up with the inconvenience of a dry mouth, and of feeling "all doped up." He can and should listen to her worries and complaints. He has to steer a middle course between excessive sympathy on the one hand and being too hard on the other. The patient should be allowed to air her views, but not all the time, or the poor man will become exhausted from listening. If he has been adequately instructed about the illness he can safely reassure her that her symptoms are all a part of her depression and that, as the doctor has said, this horrid phase will pass. Reassurance such as this needs to be repeated again and again. Depressed patients do not seem to mind such a repetition and it often helps, although at the time they seem unconvinced.

As the patient improves the situation gets a lot easier for all concerned, but it is most important to see that the illness clears completely and does not remain in a state of arrested depression. If a woman has been very depressed, and she recovers to eighty per cent of her normal vitality and state of well being, she is so grateful for having been helped, she may feel it would be churlish to complain that she is not completely well. The husband must see to it that the doctor knows the true position and the actual extent of the recovery.

This is not at all easy, and everyone cannot be as clever as a woman patient of mine. She had her second episode of depression soon after the new antidepressant drugs had become available. She was put on these tablets in full doses and made what seemed to me a very good recovery. After about three months of treatment, she was very apologetic when she saw me. She told me she was far, far better for the tablets, but still not her old self, and she just did not want to live the rest of her life twenty per cent below par. As drugs had apparently produced only this partial recovery the only possibility of further improvement appeared to be a course of E.C.T. which seemed a rather drastic undertaking, but she insisted that she was willing to have any treatment which would make her better. She was referred to a psychiatrist who, when he had talked to her, telephoned me. He felt that she was no longer depressed, certainly she was not bad enough to warrant E.C.T., but in view of the history he agreed to try the effect of a few treatments, and the patient was soon back to normal completely. She has had no relapse over the past fourteen years.

In the same way drugs may "top up" a patient who has responded well to E.C.T. but has not completely recovered. I had a patient who contracted what appeared to be a chronic anxiety state during the war. He was a hypochondriacal type and, although he was admitted to a mental hospital for six months, he had no active treatment. He improved up to a point and was sent home, but he was far from well. He managed to do his job until 1955 when he had a second episode of depression. This time he was given E.C.T. as an outpatient, and improved rapidly. He was most impressed at how quickly the clouds had lifted and felt that he was better than he had been for some years. In 1960 he had a third episode of depression and in spite of the help E.C.T. had given him, he was reluctant to admit his need for treatment again. By now antidepressive tablets were available and he was persuaded to embark on a course. After a month's treatment he remarked with delight how well he felt. He was warned that he would have to take the tablets for quite a long time. With great feeling he said he was prepared to take them for the rest of his life if necessary. He had never felt so well, nor enjoyed his work so much for twenty years. His wife confirmed this story. Ever since his troubles during the war he had found life difficult. Now he was an entirely different man on his tablets. In his first wartime depression he had sunk pretty low, but had had a spontaneous recovery which had made him sixty per cent well. Later when he had E.C.T. he was raised to the eighty per cent level, but it took the tablets to take him really to the top. They may even have put him in a mild state of productive hypomania.

If the relative feels that the doctor is not really in sympathy with the problem, or if the illness continues in spite of all the treatment, then it is probably a great deal easier for the relative than for the patient to ask for a second opinion. No good doctor minds a patient seeing a specialist, as in the complex system of medicine, where advances are being made every month, it is quite impossible for a G.P. to keep abreast in every branch of medical science. A psychiatrist is the most likely consultant to be suggested, and here again the husband can be a great comfort to his wife if he takes her to see the new doctor, and is prepared to help her out if she cannot explain what is happening. However, doctors like to get the history first hand even if the story is slow and halting, so if a relative is sitting in the same room with the patient and the doctor, he should let the patient tell her own story, and not interrupt any conversation between doctor and patient. Afterwards there should be an opportunity for the relative to explain what is happening and his version can be most useful to fill in gaps or correct inaccuracies, and the patient will usually be very glad of this help. The paranoid type of patient may make all sorts of accusations against other people which are completely untrue. One old woman became very strange. She accused the relatives who called each day to do her shopping of stealing her money and said her neighbours kept knocking on the walls to annoy her. Her husband was able to assure me that both these assertions were in fact delusions.

Relatives of patients who have recovered are relieved, but they naturally tend to worry in case the illness will recur. One must admit recurrence is very likely in some depressed patients although relapse is by no means inevitable. The situation is not helped by being fussy and over-anxious and the relative has to avoid this, without going to the opposite extreme, thereby failing to notice and report significant early symptoms. Most relatives who are really interested in the patient's welfare manage this extremely well. A few patients need to have continuous drug treatment to prevent relapse. It is a nuisance to have to take tablets all the time, but it is far better than being ill again, and sensible support from understanding relatives can be a great help.

The relatives of patients who suffer from a chronic depressive illness or hypochondriasis are in a very difficult position. In a crisis it is easy to rise to the occasion, to be sympathetic and helpful in every possible way, but with a chronic illness this tempo of service is difficult to sustain. The wells of sympathy dry up, and if a useful relationship is to survive the ordeal, the healthy partner must be in some way detached. The family have to build up a kind of immunity against the constant complaints of the patient, and care must be taken to see that no one is hopelessly trapped into becoming a helpless minion to a demanding and tyrannical hypochondriac. Time spent with, and sympathy spent on the patient must be strictly rationed, or they will be claimed in ever increasing doses. On the other hand it is only too easy to become case hardened to such a problem, and too much discipline can be almost as disastrous as giving in to every whim of the invalid. If the patient feels she is not getting her quota of attention, the symptoms become exaggerated and more urgent.

The art of living with the chronic mentally sick is to find just the right balance between sympathy and a kindly defensive insulation, but it is not easy to attain this balance and avoid a sense of guilt. Discussing the whole situation with a skilled social worker or the family doctor may help to keep the problem in perspective. Domination by the illness itself is an ever present danger, the life and interests of all the household being gradually sacrificed to its demands. If a husband lives alone with a chronically depressed wife he may on the one hand spend his entire free time keeping her company and trying to help her. He may even decide she is so ill he must give up his work to have more time for her. This wholehearted devotion, while desirable during an acute limited episode of illness, is quite wrong in the chronic state. He must be encouraged to get out and live a life of his own, not only because he needs a change, but for his wife's sake as well for, by going out to work or to the club and maintaining his own interests in life, he comes back refreshed and with local news and gossip which are the basis for everyday conversation. Excessive attentiveness can make the husband as depressed and unhappy as his melancholic partner. On the other hand there are, of course, husbands who work long hours or get out of the house at every possible opportunity, because home life has become so drear and miserable. This kind of reaction will not help the wife at home and is cruel and morally indefensible, although it may in some cases be understandable.

Even the hypochondriac who "enjoys her ill health" is mortal, and such chronic mentally sick can develop organic illness. Sometimes there may be unmistakable symptoms such as the passing of blood from some orifice in the body or a stroke, or there may simply be rather puzzling changes in the patient's behaviour to suggest an underlying physical disorder.

I remember being called to the home of a chronic depressive, having been there many many times before. On this occasion she was far less talkative and seemed somehow different, her sole complaint being of a pain in her stomach, whereas usually she had every symptom in the medical text book. She was suffering in fact from an acute appendicitis and had to go to hospital for an operation from which she made a good recovery. This episode did nothing to resolve the chronic depression which became evident once again as soon as she came home. There is, however, a real danger of organic illness being overlooked in the patient who is for ever crying "Wolf! Wolf!" and observant relations can often help by drawing the doctor's attention to a change in the pattern by furnishing some relevant observation.

Relatives often worry about what will happen to the children of depressed patients; whether they are likely to inherit the complaint and how their lives are likely to be affected by a parent's episodes of illness. There is a familial tendency with depressive illness, and this must be a source of regret, but it is as well to be reminded that depression most often arises in hard-working, clever and conscientious people. According to Sir Julian Huxley's autobiography,[4] depression certainly ran in his family, but it might well be argued this was a small price to pay for an inheritance which could at the same time produce such intellectual brilliance.

Illness of any kind in, say, the mother of children who are still at home is bound to affect their lives to some extent, but mental illness such as depression or even schizophrenia seems to be far less damaging than the fussing of a chronically anxious mother. Children seem to make allowances for episodic depression and are rarely disturbed. They are also very tolerant of the eccentricities of the schizophrenic parent. They are far more vulnerable to the suggestions and fears of someone overprotective. A depressive episode, even a severe one, is unlikely to have any long term effect upon small children.

[4] Huxley, J., *Memories* (Penguin Books, 1970).

Relatives of depressed patients, especially the next of kin, have a difficult task to perform. The husband of the depressed woman is the most important helper she has. He needs advice and moral support from the medical services, but his courage and constant attention are vital at the critical phase of the illness, and in the end when recovery has taken place he will find it wholly rewarding.

5

The Doctor's Job

MEDICAL students in the early 'thirties were taught very little psychiatry. As far as I can remember there were about six grisly sessions at the local "lunatic asylum" where patients with extreme symptoms of depression and schizophrenia were exhibited. We admired a padded cell and had a strait jacket demonstrated to us. Clinical details were much less impressed on my memory than were locked doors, the endless corridors which were constantly being scrubbed by the inmates who shuffled round in ill-fitting clothes, and the ubiquitous smell of corduroy trousers and stale food.

When I qualified I was totally unprepared for dealing with mentally ill patients. As a locum I was called out to see a poor old woman who insisted on roaming the countryside with very few clothes on. I had no idea what was wrong with her or what to do about the situation. I found many patients came to see me with complaints for which I could find no adequate explanation. I fobbed them off with some kind of medicine, but I felt very uncomfortable about my inadequacy to deal with such problems. I remember an old man coming to see me who was obviously very distressed about his bowels. I examined him carefully but could find no signs of organic disease. I referred him to a specialist and he had a barium enema, and again the findings were negative. I assured him that he had nothing to worry about, but he remained unconvinced and a few days later he gassed himself. This case left an indelible mark on my memory, but at the time the diagnosis of a senile depression had never crossed my mind.

This kind of experience in medical education is by no means

unique. Indeed, it was the common lot of medical students until about ten years ago.

At least ten per cent of the patients seen in general practice are suffering from anxiety, depression or some mental problem, but no one bothered to give us any guidance as to how to deal with this kind of case. One naturally assumed that only general practitioners had this problem and that the vast majority of patients seen at hospital level were suffering from classical organic syndromes, and therefore the teachers were unaware of the difficulty. This is not so. In two successive surveys Gottlieb[1] has shown that in new patients seen in a medical outpatient department 39 per cent and 40.2 per cent respectively had non-organic complaints. So the problem was there, but our teachers for one reason or another ignored the subject, probably because they were as ignorant as the average general practitioner as to how it should be tackled.

"Hysteria" came at the end of every differential diagnosis, but I do not remember ever being shown a hysteric : nor was there ever any instruction on how to handle such problems. Patients who failed to fit in to one of the alternative diagnoses were dismissed from the clinics with a reassuring note to the family doctor that there was "really nothing wrong with the patient." If one bears in mind this background to medical schools of that time it is really not surprising to find that there were, and still are, family doctors who do not understand this type of case, and have little sympathy for the psychiatric patient who really embarrasses them. No wonder large quantities of sedatives and sleeping tablets are dispensed. It is one way of disposing of such patients, and the advertisements which pour through the doctor's letter box assure the gullible that the latest blend of tranquillizer and antidepressant will cure all kinds of minor mental problems.

It is the minor illnesses which cause the difficulty; the patient who is seriously mentally ill can, with an easy conscience, be referred to a psychiatrist. In the worst cases all one needs to do is to sign a form and hand it over to a social worker who then

[1] Gottlieb, B. (1969), *Update*, September, p. 917.

whisks the patient into a psychiatric hospital and that is that. The suffering of the patient and her family is as far as possible repressed and forgotten.

It was quite common for medical students to be taught that they must not become emotionally involved with patients, that somehow they had to assume an attitude of detachment. This is quite reasonable for the surgeon who has a technical job to perform. A heart surgeon told me that he once interviewed some anxious parents whose small girl was to undergo a very difficult operation. At the end of the consultation the father shook him warmly by the hand and said "Do your best doctor, she is all we have." This was the last thing the surgeon wanted to know when he had a difficult mechanical task to perform. With physicians, general practitioners and psychiatrists it is different. They have not only to understand the patient, but they have to let the patient become aware that they are understood. Mentally ill patients are often surprised and comforted to learn that the doctor has sufficient empathy to know, and to be able to express, what the patient is going through. I was delighted to read that Lord Platt, one time President of the Royal College of Physicians, feels that personal involvement is essential if a complete and accurate history is to be taken from a patient.[2] A sense of sympathy is necessary for the practice of good medicine which deals with the whole man.

In the light of this historical note one hopes lay readers may perhaps have some understanding of, if not sympathy for, the doctor who appears to have little interest in this type of case. Younger doctors should be much better equipped to deal with this kind of problem. The importance of sociology, psychiatry and the common emotional problems of general practice have now been recognized and doctors in the future will be better taught and better able to deal with this kind of case. The Royal College of General Practitioners envisages the future as follows,[3] "The trainee (general practitioner) on completion of the

[2] Lord Platt, *Private and Confidential* (Cassell, 1972).
[3] Royal College of General Practitioners, *The Future General Practitioner* (British Medical Journal, 1972).

programme (of training) should be able adequately to provide personal primary and continued care to individuals and families in their homes, in his consulting room and sometimes in hospital. ... He should be able to formulate his diagnosis in physical, psychological, and social terms. He should be able to intervene educationally, preventively and therapeutically to promote his patients' health." If this comes about for the average G.P. of the future, the public will be much better served. In the past the doctor was really only interested in the physical side of medicine. Writing about these modern ways of looking at general practice, Kuenssberg wrote,[4] "The future of our patients is assured if we can train general practitioners to serve them in the ways charted here."

The sympathetic atmosphere, allowing the patient time to talk about his problems, is far more important than the mere writing of a prescription for a tranquillizer, but this approach takes longer especially when one is learning the art. One must be prepared to spend time at the beginning until skill and experience allow one to take short cuts. People work at different speeds but, whereas I used to spend hours with patients, I find now I rarely need to spend more than fifteen to twenty minutes with any psychiatric case.

The family doctor must be a good physician and a good diagnostician, but in his daily rounds he will not find many new cases of overt organic disease requiring medical or surgical treatment that seriously test his skill. A large proportion of his patients want simply to feel they are in good hands, that the doctor understands them, and to be reassured that there is nothing serious the matter. They may want to ask questions such as, "Does cancer grow from a knock?" or they may want someone to understand that the mother-in-law who now lives with them gets more impossible every week. The doctor cannot get rid of the new lodger, but by his sympathetic listening he may make the burden more tolerable and prevent tensions which could endanger health. One does not have to be in practice long before being

4 Kuenssberg, E. V., Foreword to *The Future General Practitioner* (British Medical Journal, 1972).

able intuitively to differentiate the organic illness from the psychoneurotic with considerable accuracy. This kind of intuition needs to be extended and encouraged. With practice one finds that the depressed patient has an aura of depression, the manic patient certainly infects her audience with a kind of elation, while the patient who leaves one feeling a bit bewildered is probably schizophrenic. This is, of course, an over-simplification of a complex interaction between two people, but to a greater or lesser extent such feelings are there. One of my partners once commented on an interesting and exhilarating consultation he had just finished. A very ordinary girl from the village had been holding forth on her great love of classical music amongst other things and the doctor had really enjoyed the conversation. A few weeks later she became very depressed and then it was obvious that her infectious elation stemmed from hypomania which so often is a prelude to depression. This manic phase, unrecognized at the time, had been quite arresting. We need as doctors to be more alert to the significance of our patients' moods.

Some ten to fourteen per cent of the patients who visit the doctor's surgery are suffering from what Shepherd[5] called a formal psychiatric disease. Many of these are anxious people who need time to gain confidence in their doctor, and once this has been established, the chance to talk about their troubles. Having decided from the history that the patient is suffering from a psychiatric illness, time should be given to find out why the patient is nervous, worried or depressed. The first step usually involves a complete medical examination to exclude organic illness. This formality helps the patient because she realizes her problem is being taken seriously and confidence grows. It helps the doctor, too. It is essential to exclude any organic basis for the symptoms and the behaviour of the patient during the examination is significant. The anxious patient cranes her neck to read her own blood pressure, may well point out an odd scar or pimple and by her demeanour confirm the diagnosis of anxiety. This is one of the commonest emotional problems we are

[5] Shepherd, M., Cooper, A. B., Brown, A. C. and Kalton, G. W. (1964). *British Medical Journal*, **2**, 1359.

confronted with in day-to-day practice. Once the diagnosis has been made listening to the patient is far more useful than tranquillizing tablets in the majority of cases and, with practice and patience, this does not need to take up an eternity of time.

In any medical consultation there are always two diagnoses, that of the doctor and that of the patient. If a patient attends with tonsilitis, and both the sick man and the doctor are agreed on the diagnosis, there is no problem. If the patient comes along with boils, these are lesions easy for the doctor to diagnose with certainty and to clear up with penicillin tablets. If, however, the patient is convinced the skin sepsis is in fact "syphilis coming out" which he was taught in the army could appear years later, this diagnosis of the patient must be uncovered and the whole problem sorted out if a really satisfactory recovery is to be achieved. To treat the boils and ignore the problem behind the boils is only half treatment.

It may be argued that time is far too short in a busy general practice to try and uncover such fears with every patient, but this is much easier than it sounds. Just as any experienced speaker or actor knows by some kind of intuition whether or not he is holding his audience, so the doctor can tell if he has a satisfied patient. There is no denying there are a few awkward customers, but ninety-nine per cent of patients should leave the consulting room feeling they have had the help they sought. The patient with a hidden fear is likely to ask questions : "What causes these boils doctor?", "Could I have had them in my blood for a long time?", "Do I need a blood test?" The satisfied patient with tonsilitis is unlikely to ask anything. To be sure nothing has been missed, and no question has gone unanswered, it is as well to end the interview by asking, "And is there anything else?" This does not, as some people suggest, open the flood gates of very trivial and time consuming problems. Some people need more help than others but the satisfied patient wastes little time; it is the dissatisfied client who keeps coming back and uses up many more valuable hours in the long run. Little art is needed to practise medicine with people who are always well behaved, considerate, and grateful for the doctor's help. It is a test of skill to sort out the problems of the patient who is confused, who misses her appointments, is clearly on the defensive or even frankly paranoid.

In a previous chapter, I have described the various kinds of depression. The endogenous type may not be easy to spot, but it is most gratifying to treat, and in the section which follows I shall confine my attention to this syndrome. Treatment of endogenous depression is a very important part of the doctor's job, for three very good reasons. It is very common in medical practice; it is often overlooked, and it can be the most painful and miserable experience which ever afflicts *Homo sapiens*.

THE SIZE OF THE PROBLEM

In 1971 I made a special note of all depressed patients who came my way. There are three partners in the practice and we have some 8,300 patients. With my special interest in the problem I probably see more cases than my partners but I certainly do not see all the depressions which occur. In 1971 I saw 64 new cases, 47 recurrent episodes, and 75 patients who were either on continuous treatment for depression or in a state of chronic depression.[6] During the year I thus saw some 186 cases. Depression lasts a long time. The average duration I found was seven months. This means that at every surgery one would be seeing a few cases and could expect to add about two new cases, including recurrent episodes, every week. Depression is, in fact, one of the commonest problems in medicine. Miller[7] underlining this idea wrote as follows, "Depression, like the poor, is always with us. Indeed I am often inclined to think that few of us can expect to go through life without experiencing at least one depressive episode—though whether we or our physicians will recognize its nature is another matter."

[6] Any patient under treatment for two years or more continuously was put into this category of chronic depression.
[7] Miller, H. (1967). *British Medical Journal*, **1,** 257.

Depression: The Blue Plague

THE DEPRESSION IS OFTEN OVERLOOKED

I have already described the old man who was worried about his bowels, and how I missed the basic diagnosis of senile depression. I do not think I would misdiagnose such an obvious case today, but with all my experience of the problem, the odd case still eludes me. A woman aged fifty-six came to my surgery complaining of a headache. After a complete physical examination I could find no physical basis for her problem, but, since she was not a person to complain without cause, I referred her to a physician. He too could find no organic basis, but he suggested it would be worth trying antidepressant drugs on her, and this treatment cleared her headache. She was on drugs for six months but has had none since and remains well.

To miss a mild depression like this was regrettable but not disastrous. There are, however, many horror stories about cases which have been ignored or missed. A hospital porter became very strange. He had an obsession about Russians and was always making queer remarks about them. Whenever a plane flew over the hospital he would dive under a table and his fellow porters would laugh at his antics. They did not laugh when they learned that he had murdered his wife and children "to save them from the Russians." He was detained in a special hospital during Her Majesty's pleasure, where he was given E.C.T. and recovered from his depression only to find his life in ruins. He may well have wondered bitterly why he could not have been helped much sooner especially as he had been working in a hospital.

One of my neighbours told me he had had a patient who was obsessed with the idea he was going blind. The doctor could find no real evidence of eye disease and he felt the man was excessively anxious about himself. He toyed with the idea of referring him to a psychiatrist, but then decided the patient might be offended and so sent him to an ophthalmologist. The doctor told the consultant in his letter that he was virtually sure the complaint was psychological and, if the eye specialist could not help, a psychiatric referral would be arranged. He received a letter from the consultant which was worded like this : "I have seen your patient and given him a thorough check up. Of course, as you suggested, there is nothing wrong with his eyes. I have reassured him on this score. I don't think you need worry about a psychiatrist." Unfortunately before this letter had reached the G.P. the man had committed suicide. Failure on the part of two doctors to identify the underlying depression ended in tragedy. This man appeared anxious, but not depressed. Intense anxiety is a common symptom of depression.

THE MOST PAINFUL OF HUMAN EXPERIENCES

Even mild depressions are a wretched experience, but a severe episode is sheer agony. We have potent drugs which can usually deal with physical pain and the relief does not imply that the patient is rendered unconscious. There are no comparable drugs to ease depression. Drugs take ten to fourteen days to work, E.C.T. may be quicker but relief is not immediate as is the rapid, blissful release from pain of intravenous pethidine. In addition, there are two characteristics of depression which make it particularly intractable. There is a complete absence of hope for a cure on the part of the patient and death or disaster seem inevitable. Furthermore, so often there is a tendency on the part of the patient to blame herself : she deserves to suffer because she has lived a wicked life. Patients suffering physical pain, as with terminal cancer, rarely kill themselves. Depression is the most common cause of suicide. The testimony of recovered patients bears out the utter horror induced by depression. Horder[8] told me of a woman patient of his who had had a breast removed for cancer, her gall bladder removed, and had had a severe depression all in one year. When she had recovered she was asked which was the worst experience, and she replied she would rather have the other breast off and another abdominal operation at the same time than have another depression. That was by far the worst experience. Another woman, who had failed to respond to the usual drugs and to E.C.T., was given iproniazid which cleared

[8] Horder, J. P. *Personal communication.*

her depression, but she spent several weeks in a general hospital recovering from liver damage caused by that drug. When she was discharged she was told that on no acocunt was she ever to take iproniazid again. She at once asked what was she to do if she ever became depressed again, and she was told if she took any more of that drug she would die. "I would rather die than remain depressed," was her reply.

Few people who have not experienced depression, or indeed any severe emotional upset, are really aware of how dreadful the patient feels. Forty years ago, when there was no treatment for this illness, perhaps the profession could be forgiven for turning a blind eye to the problem. None of us enjoy being confronted by an incurable malady. Today there is no such excuse.

The Protean Syndrome

Before there was any treatment for it, syphilis was always acclaimed as the master mimic of organic diseases. With its sores, rashes, lumps and neurological manifestations it could be found in almost every branch of medicine. Nevertheless, at least the diagnosis could be confirmed by a blood test, but there are no such convenient tests for endogenous depression which can also appear in many forms, and this is why the diagnosis is so often missed. The various types are listed below.

The Severe Psychotic Depression. This form of depression is striking and obvious, and in a book of this kind it needs no detailed description. The patient may be so retarded she can hardly speak but her misery is written across her face, or she may be so agitated that she cannot sit still but wanders about wringing her hands. The case with depressive delusions may not be quite so obvious. If the patient talks about them, and says he has venereal disease and is infecting the whole neighbourhood, the diagnosis is clear, but if he keeps them to himself, like the man who was worried about his eyesight, it is not so easily recognized. The patient who is convinced she has organic disease when there are clearly no physical signs to support this contention is far more likely to be depressed than anxious. The "smiling depression" is another dangerous type, which is not very common, but a smiling face can indeed mask a severe and dangerous depression.

Anxiety and Depression. Manifest anxiety is far and away the commonest cloak for covert depression. If one considers how the illness develops the reason becomes obvious. Few depressions come on overnight and the onset is usually slow and insidious. The first symptom is likely to be a falling off of energy which can be quite marked. For a short time the patient may argue she is tired because she has been overdoing things, but after two or three weeks this kind of explanation fails to satisfy. The patient then begins to think along one of two lines. She either feels she is "getting neurotic" and heading for a complete nervous breakdown, or she thinks she has some lethal organic disease like cancer, tuberculosis or poliomyelitis. Whatever her thoughts, she becomes very anxious about herself, so that anxiety is an early symptom of depression, and may well occur before obvious depressive symptoms. In fact it is only after the phase of anxiety has lasted for some time that a "depressive threshold" is reached. Thereafter the patient becomes weepy and dispirited, there is a marked sleep disturbance and she is obviously depressed. The depressive episode can end at any stage of this progression. Periodic attacks of anxiety can be a series of mild depressions which have never passed the depressive threshold, so that the paradoxical situation obtains where the patient is suffering from a depression but does not feel depressed. Only a very small proportion of cases sink to the nadir and become psychotic. If a patient is suffering from unexplained anxiety, depression should be suspected; if the anxiety is severe it is almost certainly depression.

A youth of nineteen came to see me with a pain in his chest. I could find no signs of organic disease so I referred him to a chest physician. His X-ray was clear, there were no pathogens in the sputum, and the physician in his letter concluded that the man's anxiety was so intense that it suggested depression. This was indeed an excellent diagnosis. He was given antidepressant drugs and his symptoms cleared.

Confronted by a patient who is anxious, a search should be made for the cause. If no cause is obvious, or if the explanation given by the patient is clearly false, as for instance the middle-aged man who blames his symptoms on the memory of stealing a valuable postage stamp from a school friend thirty years before, treatment for depression should be given. If there is any doubt about the diagnosis treatment should be initiated. Antidepressant drugs do no harm to the anxious patient, but to treat depression as anxiety can end in disaster.

Depression disguised as organic disease. The emotional control centre in the hypothalamus lies close to the control centres of the autonomic nervous system. An upset of one centre can easily, as it were, overflow into the other so that the depressed patient is afflicted with many physical symptoms such as a fast pulse, indigestion, abdominal distension, sweating and pain in almost any form. In a series of 585 cases, pain was the presenting symptom in twenty-nine per cent.[9] The disguise can be very convincing. Many years ago now I was confronted by a patient with a distended abdomen which I was sure was an intestinal blockage. I referred her to hospital where an exploratory operation was done but no organic lesion found. The patient recovered from the operation and on her return home the diagnosis was clearly one of depression. She had had a previous episode accompanied by suicidal ideas, and she has since had further attacks which have responded well to drugs.

Another case of mine is well worth relating as it raises so many interesting facets of the subject. A man aged fifty came to see me with a bad cough and loss of weight. He looked very ill and felt dreadful so he was referred to a chest clinic where a small suspicious shadow was found on his chest X-ray, and carcinoma of the lung was suspected. No further investigations were carried out. Biopsy and sputum analysis were not available as diagnostic aids in those days. As expected he deteriorated and I felt the end

[9] Watts, C. A. H., *Depressive Disorders in the Community* (Wright, 1966).

84

could not be far away. On one visit to his home, however, his wife told me that before his illness had started, he had gone through a very strange period. An indolent man by nature, he had become hyperactive. He had taken to getting up early in the morning to garden, and was full of silly ideas such as wishing to adopt children. If crossed he became angry and on one occasion had actually struck his wife, a thing he had never done in his life before. With uncanny clinical accuracy this simple country woman concluded, "I thought he was getting the mania." On the strength of this remark he was X-rayed once more. The shadow had not changed and it was now suggested it could well be a healed tubercular focus. A psychiatrist was called in and the diagnosis of depression was confirmed. He was transferred to a mental hospital where he was given E.C.T. and made a good recovery.

There are a number of lessons to be learned from this story. Even with my interest in the subject I missed the diagnosis. The importance of getting a history from the next of kin is underlined : but for the story of his hypomania he could certainly have died. Lastly, even very ill patients who have wasted away can make a good recovery with E.C.T.

If one is in doubt as to whether or not the patient has an organic disease or depression, the former must be excluded before steps are taken to deal with depression. Treatment of an organic lesion, where it exists, will in all probability clear up the depressive symptoms, but sometimes both illnesses need to be treated at the same time. Diseases of the thyroid gland are liable to cause depression and, on more than one occasion, in order to secure complete recovery, both the gland malfunction and depression have had to be treated side by side.

The Depressive Graft. Chronic organic illness affords no immunity to depression, rather the reverse. The patient suffering from chronic bronchitis, rheumatism or even a broken leg can contract a depression which is grafted on to the illness making it appear that the basic condition is deteriorating. A man who had had chronic bronchitis for years, became sure his last day had come. He could not sleep at nights, his cough was more trying than ever, and he wished his sufferings were over. A course of antidepressant drugs did him a great deal of good, and he recovered his usual cheerful attitude to his illness. Similarly, I remember seeing an old woman at a London hospital who was confined to bed with a broken neck of femur. She had become more and more morose, refusing her food, and a psychiatrist was called in to see her. E.C.T. was given to her, and she became much more her old self and was able to face up to the tedium of convalescence.

Old people are very prone to depression, and all too often it is assumed that their symptoms are just part and parcel of senescence, and something which is inevitable and has to be endured. It should not be forgotten that even senile depressions are often alleviated by drugs, or E.C.T. if necessary.

Chronic illness is very much a part of general practice. Sudden new symptoms or deterioration of the condition may be due to a depressive graft, and at least this possibility should be borne in mind. Depressive grafts are not confined to chronic disease. Post-influenzal depression is such a graft, and this sort of thing can happen with any illness.

Behaviour disturbances. This is an unusual form of presentation, but every practice must have a few cases. There is a sudden inexplicable departure from a normal pattern of behaviour. The first case I had of this kind was in the army, when a man suffering from delirium tremens came under my care. With intensive vitamin therapy he soon recovered from his terrifying hallucinations. His history was that for months he had felt run down and wretched, and had had great difficulty in sleeping. He found it increasingly difficult to meet people until he discovered that a liberal dose of brandy made quite a difference to his feelings, and with several doubles inside him his insomnia vanished. He had never been in the habit of taking alcohol, and his wife affirmed that he was not a drinker. Fortunately by the time the delirium tremens had been dealt with, the depression too had passed, so he made a good recovery all round. Here depression manifested itself by turning a normally temperate man into a drunkard.

Two similar cases of behaviour disturbances as the overt symptom of depressive illness came to my attention, again both involving hitherto normal middleaged men, one of whom suddenly became an obsessive gambler and the other fell foul of the law by becoming an exhibitionist. Both responded well to conventional treatment for depression. Cases of this kind are tragic, because the character and reputation of a respectable citizen can be shattered by a stupid impulsive act, perpetrated in a state of depression. Overspending, shop-lifting, and bizarre sexual aberrations may all occur during a depressive mood swing, and it is little consolation to learn one has been suffering from a treatable illness when one has appeared before the courts and had one's name splashed in the local papers. The tendency is to think that the depression is a result of the aberrant behaviour and the public and private humiliation it brings when, in fact, the reverse is the case. It is the depression which causes the strange behaviour.

RECOGNITION OF A DEPRESSIVE ILLNESS

There is unfortunately no blood test or X-ray examination which will clinch the diagnosis of depression in the same way that one can confirm a case of syphilis by finding a positive blood reaction or tuberculosis by X-ray. The most important aid to diagnosis is to have the possibility of such an illness in mind. If the condition is suspected and the patient has no overt worries which could have caused it, and there is no evidence of anaemia, diabetes or other possible organic disease, then the patient should be questioned along the following lines, looking at five groups of symptoms.[10] The patient need not have them all but three or four are usually present even in the mildest case.

(1) Decline in Energy. As already mentioned, one of the earliest symptoms is a falling-off of energy. The patient finds herself less and less able to cope with the housework and one glance at the

[10] Watts, C. A. H., *Update*. In the press.

untidy home of an erstwhile house-proud woman may clinch the diagnosis. Discussing this decline in energy with a psychiatrist and a highly intelligent patient who had suffered recurrent depressions was of interest. The psychiatrist felt that this mild type of case could possibly be cured by light diversions such as golf, or going out to dinner and so on. The patient thought otherwise : "By a great effort of will I can keep to the routine jobs I know about, I have no drive left for anything new." The housewife looks at the stairs and wonders how she can ever summon the energy to mount them. The "regular pint" man stops drinking, as by nightfall he has not sufficient energy to go down to the local.

(2) Disturbance of the Sleep Rhythm. Textbooks usually describe early morning waking as typical of endogenous depression. This may indeed be so, but any sleep upset can occur in this illness. The patient may be so anxious he cannot fall asleep, or sleep is fitful all night. He may blame physical symptoms such as pain or a cough for keeping him awake. On the other hand he may sleep far more than he used to do. He can go to bed early, sleep the clock round, only to waken as unrefreshed as if he had had no sleep. Morning lethargy is a typical depressive symptom. All patients with this illness have some disturbance of their sleep rhythm. If the patient claims to sleep well, it is worth questioning the spouse who may well think otherwise. One man had to get out of bed and climb in on the other side, because his wife was so restless at night, although she claimed to sleep well.

(3) Mood Swings. The classical picture is to "feel awful" in the mornings and almost normal towards nightfall, but any variation is possible. I have had one patient who felt fine when she awakened, and dreaded nightfall. This swing of mood is pathognomonic of depression and it is a very disconcerting experience when hopes and fears alternate for weeks on end. It is one of the factors which keeps the patient away from her doctor. When she is down she decides she will see her physician, but she cannot summon up the energy to go straight away. Later in the day, when she feels so much better, what can she tell her doctor?

There seems no need to go at all, and so a consultation is evaded again and again.

(4) Habit Changes. These are typical of the depressed patient. They are usually far more evident to the family than the doctor, and this is why relatives should be advised to report any suspicion of a recurrent episode. The neglected home or untidy garden in a family with reasonable standards may spell depression in a wife or husband. The regular drinker gives it up, or drinks to excess, which is out of character with his normal way of life. All the appetites tend to alter : the patient usually eats less but some eat too much. Sex becomes taboo to many. A few have an increased libido which worries them a great deal, so that there is little pleasure in the new way of life. The family doctor has a big advantage over any consultant psychiatrist in that he is familiar with the normal behaviour of his patients. He may see warning signs in the facial expression or in diminished muscle tone. The usually active man slumps into his seat in the consulting room and is lost for words to say how he feels. The patient may become more religious, going to Mass daily instead of once a week. One Catholic patient of mine, who had married a Protestant twenty years before in a registry office, insisted on being remarried in church, believing that she was not properly married. The conscience is so much more sensitive in this state that peccadilloes of the past are resurrected and become painful obsessions. The missionary box which was opened to buy fireworks thirty years before begins to prey on a patient's mind day and night.

(5) Depression. If it is decided that the patient is depressed it is very important to gauge the depth of depression, and once the patient realizes he is talking to a doctor who understands, this is not difficult. I ask my patient "Do you feel depressed?" A denial does not exclude this illness, as early cases can feel worried and anxious without actually being depressed, as I have already stated.

Most patients, however, will agree they do feel down and depressed. I then ask the patient "How depressed do you feel?" This rarely produces any answer, but makes him begin to think, so after a short time I ask "Do you feel fed up?" The patient usually admits he is fed up, and so I ask him "How fed up do you feel?" Again there is rarely an immediate answer to this question, and after a pause I ask "Do you feel life is hardly worth living?" This invariably produces a response. The patient either denies such feelings and says, "I am not as bad as that," or he agrees he has felt that way. With the patient who admits to such feelings I go on to ask "Have you ever felt like taking your own life?" If the patient admits to suicidal ideas, I ask him if he has actually worked out ways and means of committing suicide. If he has done so he is quite near to the act and in urgent need of help.

To discuss this with a patient always helps and the patient with suicidal ideas feels better for having discussed the matter. It is, however, advisable to secure psychiatric help for such patients, but this must be done without any sense of panic. There must, in fact, be no precipitate action as this will alarm the patient and he may well feel that the doctor is rejecting him. I tell the patient who had admitted to suicidal ideas that such symptoms are a measure of how bad he must have felt. I tell him how wise he has been to seek help and with treatment he will soon feel a great deal better.

Two patients have warned me that they really did not feel responsible for their actions when in this frame of mind, and both were relieved to be admitted at once to a psychiatric hospital. Others I see at frequent intervals for a while, daily if necessary, and then tell the patient I have given his problem a lot of thought and have decided a psychiatric colleague will be able to help more than I can. A domiciliary visit can be most helpful with such cases. Handed over tactfully and in an unhurried way ensures that the patient doctor rapport will carry over to the consultant.

MANAGEMENT

The management of the depressed patient consists of supportive therapy and physical measures of treatment. The supportive measures start as soon as the patient realizes that his problem is being taken seriously and that the doctor really does understand how he feels. The way questions are asked, the way replies are received and interpreted, must all encourage confidence. The patient who hardly understands himself, who has probably been told at home and at work that he must pull himself together, is greatly relieved to be told he has done the right thing in coming to see the doctor, and that he really does need help to get better. He is told that this type of illness is very common and much is known about it. It is physical as an attack of pneumonia. This type of patient has been likened to a traveller in a foreign land who has got lost; suddenly he finds someone who speaks his language and who can direct him back on to the right road. His relief and gratitude for such help is considerable. Simple repetitive supportive measures are all that is needed.

When I was taught psychiatry twenty-eight years ago, I was told that psychotherapy was dangerous to this type of patient, and there is some truth in this view. To dig into the past and to try and explain symptoms in terms of psychopathology could waste hours of time and the patient was rarely helped (or impressed). Indeed he could feel that the treatment was quite futile, and this thought could make him feel more hopeless than ever. What these patients really need is a confident, supportive understanding. "I know how awful you feel, but this phase will pass. In a week or two you will feel quite different." This kind of reassurance may have to be repeated again and again. The patient may well not believe the doctor at the time, but, nevertheless, the confident understanding of the therapist is a great help.

All doctors feel a bit irritated by some of the chronic psychoneurotics in their practices, but with a new case this should never happen. No matter how stupid or bizarre the symptoms, the patient should have his problem treated seriously and with respect. If he is depressed he may well have screwed up all his courage to come along. If he feels snubbed, or is told to pull himself together, he may never seek medical advice again and continue to suffer on his own until after months a remission sets in, or he may take his own life. The medical profession as a whole seems to equate the psycho-neurotic syndromes with non-urgent trivia, an attitude which is wholly unrealistic and cruel. Acute and severe anxiety or depression, no matter what the cause, constitute medical emergencies and should be treated as such. The basis of the worry may be physical, such as the discovery of a lump in the breast, or it may be from a depressive delusion. In either case steps should be taken to see that the problem is treated as a matter of urgency. To make the patient feel he is wasting the doctor's time, or that he is creating a fuss about nothing, is very poor medicine.

The next step is to tell the patient how he is going to be treated. If work is too much for him, he should be advised to go sick and take a few weeks sick leave. This often helps, as it is easier to put up with the side effects from drugs at home than at work. He is told that he will not get better overnight, but that in two or three weeks he should feel vastly different. In order to assess his reaction to the drugs he should be seen at least twice a week in the first place. As soon as improvement is apparent, this interval can be extended.

PHYSICAL MEASURES OF TREATMENT

Endogenous depression is a self-limiting illness, and most cases get better in time with or without treatment. In the days when I used to spend long sessions with my patients, recovery was sometimes attributed to psychotherapy when in fact an unrecognized depression had cleared.

I remember a woman I saw in 1946 who was depressed, and I felt the basis of her problem was that her husband, a lorry driver, worked very irregular hours. I discussed her problems at length and she improved. Four years later she had a very severe depression necessitating admission to a mental hospital for E.C.T. and after another four years she had a similar episode. Looking back, I feel sure that when I first saw her she was at the end of a depressive episode, and my therapy was virtually no more than a supportive measure. Her husband did not change his job or his way of life and yet she recovered.

With this knowledge of a possible remission in mind, and faced with a very mild case of depression, I see the patient regularly, discuss any problems which may have arisen, and prescribe vitamin tablets. I do not prescribe either minor tranquillizers or hypnotics, for reasons stated in an earlier chapter. It is so easy to start a patient off on these drugs, and so difficult to stop them and, in addition, they often merely obscure the issue. One may suggest that a patient takes aspirins to relieve toothache, but it is far better medicine to deal radically with the lesion in the tooth. I feel there is no place for sedatives in the treatment of depression.

On the other hand, in my view the antidepressant drugs are as valuable in psychiatry as are the antibiotics in the management of infectious diseases. Just as antibiotics are not used to treat a pimple so antidepressant drugs should not be used hastily to treat an early, mild depression. If however the illness has lasted a long time, or if the symptoms are severe, then I am prepared to start at once on drug treatment.

Tricyclic Drugs. This group consists of imipramine, amitriptyline, and allied drugs. If the patient is suffering from insomnia of any kind, this is the drug of choice. By giving a large dose at night, no hypnotic is necessary. People vary widely in their tolerance of the drug. Some patients feel drowsy on a small dose; others can take an enormous quantity and feel no ill effect. The starting dose depends on how the patient is situated. If she is a woman with young children to care for, or he is a man who wants to carry on with his job, then small doses are indicated, but it is likely to take longer for them to feel better. It takes ten to twenty days before a change occurs. When it does come, the patient should feel vastly better: it is not just a question of a marginal improvement. "I am so much better I now realize how ill I was," is the kind of remark I like to hear.

If the patient is very ill and cannot go to work in any case and it does not really matter if she does sleep all day for a few days, she can be given maximum doses from the start. In such a case I warn the patient that she will feel side effects such as a

93

dry mouth, giddiness when she stands up, blurred vision and so on. She may feel very dopey and quite wretched for a few days, but, if she can put up with this inconvenience, it will soon pass and she is likely to feel better sooner than if the smaller dosage had been given. Once the patient has returned to normal, the daytime dose can often be reduced. Some take all their tablets at night at this stage.

The commonest mistakes with these drugs is to give too small a dose, or not to continue them long enough. Most patients have improved after two weeks but a few take longer.

Monoamine Oxidase Inhibitors. When these drugs were first used there were a number of frightening side effects, but since it has been found that these were due to a food incompatibility the alarming symptoms have almost disappeared from clinical practice. The main foods to be avoided are cheese, marmite, fish roes, red wines and broad beans, especially the pods. Morphia and the synthetic opiates should not be given. A card containing a list of these items can be obtained from the drug firms, and every patient prescribed M.A.O. drugs should be given such a card. If these simple precautions are observed, then the M.A.O. drugs are quite safe and can be very useful indeed. The first indication for this agent is the depressed patient who sleeps too much : the patient who goes to bed early, sleeps the clock round, but still awakens exhausted. She may have a few sleeps in the day for good measure. Such heavy sleepers often find that after a few days on M.A.O. drugs they develop insomnia, in which case a sedative can be prescribed at night.

Many more of my patients are on the amitriptyline group of drugs, but I have had some of the most striking recoveries by employing M.A.O. drugs, especially in the arrested type of depression. A woman was admitted to a mental hospital during the war because of psychiatric upset. She must have felt very ill to have agreed to the admission. She improved and was discharged and I met her in 1947. She was a pleasant person, but very nervous, always expecting the worst to happen. She tended to stay at home, and got in a state if she went out. Nothing I could do had much effect on her, but in 1958 when imipramine became available I tried her on this drug, and she improved considerably. When tranylcypromine came along, I switched to this and the transformation was dramatic. She felt better than she had done since her admission to the mental hospital in 1943. She started to go out, she joined the Women's Institute, found she could go to church without any difficulties and, from being a semi-hermit in her home, she became an active member of the community. After a year of treatment she reduced the dosage, but still has one tablet a day. She had had the drug long before the adverse effects of some food were known, and she eats what she likes.

If a patient with depression does not respond to drugs, then a psychiatric opinion should be sought. Electro convulsive therapy may well be necessary. This treatment is a completely painless procedure, and is quite safe. It often succeeds in lifting a depression when other means have failed, but its administration is in the hands of the hospital psychiatrist. Out-patient clinics for this treatment have been set up in most parts of the country and admission to hospital is rarely necessary.

Finally, patients with depression can be very illogical in their ideas. They blame all sorts of things for their symptoms. In 1949 a farmer moved into this area. He came to see me and I found him in a state of abject depression. He blamed the climate, an inconvenient house, and the loneliness. He was very keen to sell his farm, and to get right away from things. I persuaded him to see a psychiatrist and have E.C.T. I told him if after treatment he still wanted to sell his farm, he could do so. He made a good recovery and still lives in this area. If he had sold up he would have wasted a lot of money. It is surely part of the doctor's duty to prevent patients from acting on impulse or taking important decisions while they are depressed. Serious mistakes can be made under the influence of the blue plague.

Something like ninety to ninety-five per cent of depressed patients can be treated by their family doctor, and there is no need to seek hospital aid. Few patients in the whole of medicine are more grateful than the depressive patient who has been successfully treated.

6

The Doctor's Partners

A HUNDRED years ago the general practitioner tended to work alone in splendid isolation. He visited the fevers, he dispensed his own medicines, he set fractures, he delivered babies. He even pulled teeth for as little as a shilling a time, and tonsils were removed in the surgery for a guinea. There was, of course, no anaesthetic! He had no trained assistants from other disciplines.

Today his position is very different. He is a member of a team of trained personnel. He has little to do in the way of surgery but it is virtually impossible for a modern family doctor to confine his work to that of the physician. To cover the ground adequately entails involvement in the other two closely related spheres of psychological and social medicine. For example, besides being able to deal with anxiety states and cases of depression, he must be an expert in family planning, even if he does not fit caps or insert loops.

He is, in fact, consulted about all kinds of things which are not strictly medical. A child has school phobia and says she is frightened of the bigger girls: what can be done to make it easier for her? The eldest son has been dismissed from his work because he was caught stealing: what can the parents do? Father at fifty has been made redundant and is taking it very badly. He will not even look for another job and his unemployment benefit is not enough to live on. Sometimes the family doctor can himself help to sort out the problem, but often he will be well advised to hand it over to a social worker in his team.

A woman of forty-nine had for some years cared for her ageing parents. Her mother died first, and years later her father. She had no income of her own and she had not put stamps on to her National Insurance card. She was a quiet gentle creature who was temperamentally unfitted at forty-nine to go out and find a job. Who could advise us how to help her? The health visitor at once suggested a phone call to the Social Security office, and one of their officers came to her rescue and sorted the problems out.

In the following pages, an attempt is made to show how the nursing services, the health visitors and office staff can play an effective part in the detection, treatment and prevention of the blue plague.

The District Nurse and Midwife

These two functions are now sometimes carried out by different nursing sisters, but their roles in social medicine can be considered together. Ever since their institution in 1901 they have been our closest allies in general practice and we have the highest regard for them. Until recently they have worked more or less on their own, but now the trend is for attachment systems and provided that this is based on the idea of partnership, rather than just an extra pair of hands from "the doctors' handmaid," the concept has great advantage to both parties.

This book is no place to discuss the everyday work of the nursing services, but only in so far as they can help us in the problem of dealing with the blue plague. To be of real value here, they must be aware of the problem, and they must have easy access to the doctor to discuss any difficulty that arises, large or small. They must be able to reach him at his surgery, or by telephone at any time, or at the bedside of the patient. Knowing the nursing sister makes all the difference. A call for help or co-operation from a practice nurse creates an immediate and willing response on the part of the doctor. The situation is totally different when an unknown factory nurse sends some casualty home from work and puts a message in for the doctor to call. This can quite irrationally cause considerable irritation, even if the call is completely justifiable. Nobody likes to be told what to do, or to be given extra work by a complete stranger.

Until quite recently the district nurse and the midwife were referred to as Nurse, or more affectionately as "Our Nurse." Today there is a hierarchy of nursing staff helping the family doctor. At the top is the fully qualified state registered nurse (S.R.N.) and the state certified midwife (S.C.M.). These workers are quite properly called Sisters. They are assisted by state enrolled nurses (S.E.N.), who are directed by the Sister in charge. Finally there are nursing auxiliaries who do not perform the skilled nursing duties. They wash and bed bath the aged and chronic invalids at regular intervals. It is very important that these workers should be known by their proper titles. The label "Sister Smith" carries with it a status which is lacking in the term "Mrs. Smith." With the title of Sister, or for the junior ranks Nurse, the patient realizes that she is being treated by an expert, and not just some kind-hearted neighbour.

Most general practitioners are men, and most of the nursing staff are women, and this sexual difference can be very valuable. I am conscious that, because of my maleness, I usually have a bias in favour of the woman. For instance, I was consulted by a pair whose marriage was breaking up. The man I felt was paranoid, he had queer ideas about his wife and her fidelity was suspect. The woman told me that, because of his attitude, she felt she had no more affection for him, could not bear him near her, and I understood her feelings. It was a woman social worker who was helping me on the case who discovered that the woman had taken to sleeping downstairs to get away from her husband at night. Her reaction was much more practical than mine and less sympathetic : "No wonder your husband thinks you have a lover, if you deliberately avoid him. In a situation such as this if you really want to save the marriage, no matter what your feelings at the moment, you must make up to him, and show him you do really want his attentions and affection." This approach was appreciated and accepted by the woman, and the social worker's intervention in this case was far more realistic and helpful than mine.

In general, however, the doctor is the rather intimidating father figure and the nurse the kindly and more approachable mother figure, often consulted on problems she can deal with on her own, sometimes far better than the doctor. The nursing sister visits homes, and today home visiting is falling out of favour among doctors as people are encouraged to use the surgery where more equipment and better diagnostic facilities are available. The eye of a woman picks up more details of the home than the average man, and she may well spot items which are significant— the erstwhile tidy house which is becoming unkempt, the children who are snapped at and in general less well cared for, dirty and ill clad. The nursing sister with the listening ear will receive many confidences which can relieve the anxious mother. If she feels the problem is too difficult or out of her province it can easily be referred back to the family doctor.

The district midwife is in an admirable situation to discuss problems of pregnancy which the young mother may feel too trivial for the doctor but can cause a lot of anxiety, or there may be subjects which embarrass her and which are easier to discuss with another woman. The various types of depression which occur after childbirth have already been described, and the midwife should be an expert at dealing with the "fourth day blues." She should also be on her guard to spot the warnings of a more sinister depression, the acute insomnia, inappropriate questions, such as, "Is it really my baby?" or, from a delivered woman with a nice flat abdomen, "Am I really having twins?" The family may well treat such remarks as a joke, or they may be so upset by the occasional incoherence of the patient, or her hallucinations or delusions, that they ignore them, hoping that they will pass. To the midwife such aberrations are highly significant and will be reported to the doctor at once. Such symptoms are much more likely to be shown while she is making the mother comfortable or bathing the baby, than when the doctor calls for a much shorter visit. The more insidious, post-puerperal depressions are not likely to come to her notice, as this syndrome becomes evident later when she has finished with her patient.

Terminal nursing can be a tiring, dirty and repulsive task for any nurse, but in no other situation can she do more good, not only for the patient, but for the entire family. The experience calls not only on her highest nursing ability, but also on her maternal instincts. All sick people regress towards childhood and, in a sense, the helpless wet and dirty body on the death bed is in a second childhood. One young nurse surprised me by saying that she felt her most rewarding experience was when in hospital she nursed a woman who was dying. In the course of the two weeks before the patient's death she grew close to both the patient and the family, and both depended on her. No nurse, or doctor, for that matter, counted as much, and she must have given tremendous support to the relatives who often feel so impotent in such a situation. Her daily contacts and talks would have gone far to ease some of the problems of mourning once the end had come.

Routine nursing activities are only one section of work for the nurse in general practice. Her duties cover a far wider spectrum than her counterpart in hospital. For example, she may well have to organize clean bed linen ready for her next visit, and the family or neighbours have to be encouraged to do a daily wash. Clean bedsheets do not come automatically from an inexhaustable hospital linen store. She may have to instruct the family on diets for the patient. She keeps an eye on the drugs to see that they are being taken as instructed. If the patient is in pain she will see to it that there is a supply of pain relieving drugs. She does not just look to the patient, she surveys the whole situation and takes any necessary action.

The Health Visitor

Initiated in Salford in 1921, the whole idea of the health visitor was to have an expert in the community who could practise preventive medicine. She is at her best with mothers and young children, and she knows more about infant feeding than most general practitioners. She begins her work on a family at the point when the district midwife leaves off, visiting the mother in her own home as well as seeing her at welfare clinics and helping in many different ways. After the excitement and trauma of the birth of the child the young mother receives the daily help and attention of the midwife for ten days but after that, with husband back at work, may find herself very much alone in our modern society.

For countless generations young mothers have had help and company at least for a month from mother or mother-in-law, or from a nanny if she were rich. In small communities there may be friends and visitors to call but in large conurbations a young mother can be marooned in a high rise flat with an eternally long day and a terrifying responsibility for her new arrival. The strain of such a situation is shown by the admission by a young woman doctor of her somewhat irrational delight and relief at the visit of a health visitor after her discharge from hospital with her first baby and the feeling of security it gave her, although in normal times she would expect the health visitor to lean on her.

At a conference in Canada in 1969 the view was expressed that some kind of social worker was really needed in the community to support the young mother between the time when she was under the care of the obstetrician and before she began to lean on the paediatrician, and this is exactly one of the health visitor's functions. Some people have questions to be answered and all kinds of small problems to be discussed, and this is surely one of the best ways of ensuring that the everyday trivia which puzzle do not have time to be magnified into crises. The eagerness and freedom with which many young mothers talk to health visitors demonstrates the importance of this part of their work. It is real preventive medicine taking place at a very vulnerable point in the life of the young mother. At infant welfare clinics there are no fewer than three therapeutic agencies. The health visitor herself is there to answer questions or to give advice, she has a medical colleague with whom she can consult, and finally the group of women together help each other by exchanging problems and experiences.

The health visitor also gives positive health teaching through Parent Craft classes and talks to mothers in the realm of both physical and emotional development, and in this way makes an important contribution to the prevention of the blue plague. In her visits to homes she can learn and teach a lot from what she sees. Accident hazards can be pointed out. Fire guards are often

not where they should be. Medicines and tablets are rarely locked
away. Dunnell[1] in her survey found secure medicine cabinets
were only used in 2 out of 686 households. Practical advice on
such subjects may well lead on to discussion of emotional problems. People are more confident and ready to talk in their own
homes, and in the informal atmosphere of the home the health
visitor is in an excellent position to uncover the mild depression
which frequently follows childbirth, and to persuade the mothers
to seek treatment.

A second interest of the health visitor is care of the aged, and
in this section of the community many are sad, lonely or feel
neglected, and depression in various forms thrives. One of the
best antidotes to the blues in old age is to keep active as long as
possible. The health visitor should encourage outings to Darby
and Joan Clubs, and organize as much help in the home as is
needed. Relatives may have to be visited, and actively persuaded
to assist as much as possible. Where there are no children or
relatives to help, Home Helps or Meals on Wheels may be
organized. The old person may be rendered more mobile by
adequate chiropody care, and her morale may be raised by a
visit to the hairdresser. For those who are housebound or even
chair bound by such illnesses as rheumatism or a stroke, life can
be made happier and more active by the use of all kinds of aids
and gadgets. Certain aspects of the house may need to be modi-
fied. A doorway may be too narrow to allow the passage of a
wheel chair. This may have to be widened and a ramp at the
front door installed so that the chair can easily be taken outside.
This sort of help, which requires structural alterations, can
usually be secured through the good offices of the Department
of Social Services who can arrange for the appropriate workmen
to do it. Scores of helpful items are available from the Red Cross,
which hires them out at a nominal rental, or waives any charge
if the patient cannot afford a fee.

Mental activity is as important as physical. A health visitor
found an old woman's eyesight was so bad she could no longer

[1] Dunnell, K. and Cartwright A., *Medicine Takers, Prescribers and Hoarders* (Routledge and Kegan Paul 1972).

read or watch television. She was becoming noticeably demented and could not tell the day of the week or recognize callers. If told who the visitor was, she soon forgot. An eye test was arranged and bilateral cateracts were found. The family rallied to help and the old woman was sent to see an eye specialist who agreed to operate. I myself felt it really a futile exercise, as she was so disorientated. She had her operation and it was successful, but in hospital she was so confused she was quite a problem. On her return home, however, she improved and, with a return of vision and an interest in life, her mental state improved far more than I ever expected. The removal of disabilities, even by some fairly major operation, can pay off. A prematurely old man with severe arthritis had had a number of small strokes and the outlook was black indeed. He had a new metal hip inserted and as soon as he was mobile and free from hip pain his general condition improved remarkably. He looked a good deal younger a year after his operation than he had done before this major reconstruction was attempted. Not all such manoeuvres end in success, but age itself is not a bar to major surgery or E.C.T.

A third and very important function of the health visitor is that of being a liaison officer between her general practitioners and all the other branches of the social services. The modern health visitor is trained to know how to get everything which is needed. The average family doctor is not acquainted with all the intricacies of social services in the modern world, and here the health visitor can be of the greatest help to him. She can also act as a liaison officer in other ways. She can actually visit the local school to discuss a case of school phobia with the staff. This is often of more help than a short chat on the telephone between a doctor and the head teacher. In our area the health visitor and the headmaster of the local school work in very close liaison, greatly to the benefit of the young people under their care.

THE RECEPTIONIST

Here is another very important member of the general practice team who is not a trained social worker, but nevertheless plays an important part in the running of the practice. She needs to have many of the talents of the social worker. Most people are a bit nervous when they go to see the doctor, especially if it is a first visit. Consider once more the case of a woman who is depressed. She feels guilty about wasting the doctor's time, she wonders how she will describe her feelings, and she has only agreed under duress to make the appointment. What happens on the telephone or at the reception desk can make or mar the consultation. If she is made to feel that the doctor is dreadfully busy, and it is going to be very difficult to fit her in that day, she will not relax as quickly when she does see him as when an appointment has been made without any fuss. The myth of the busy general practitioner is one of the most damaging facets of the image of the family physician today. With appointment systems, group practices and rota systems, practice nurses and adequate ancillary help, there is no excuse for appearing to be constantly in a rush. The picture of the tired, overworked general practitioner should be a relic of the past, except perhaps at the height of an influenza epidemic. With all the modern advances in general practice the man who is always in a hurry, who has insufficient time to let his patient speak before writing out a prescription or ending the consultation, is either badly organized in his practice, or he is spending too much time on the golf course.[2] The average patient does not want an eternity of time but does dislike being hurried.

I have stressed this point, because the attitude of the doctor is bound to be reflected on the receptionist's work. This member of staff has the very difficult task of satisfying the patient, and at the same time doing her best to protect her doctor from unnecessary work and pressures. Like the doctor himself she has to use some clinical judgement as to the urgency of the case and, at the same time, she must give moral support to the inquirer who is already anxious. She has, in fact, across the counter to conduct a preliminary consultation, and this requires calmness, tact and considerable skill. Her task is quite impossible if the

[2] Watts, C. A. H. (1972). *World Medicine*. Annual Review, February, p. 31.

doctor is too rigid about practice rules. Everyone makes mistakes and the receptionist should be able without fear or embarrassment to ask her doctor to see an extra patient who has come on the wrong day, or who has been wrongly booked by the office staff. If the system is to work smoothly and efficiently, the lines of communication between the doctor and his staff must be very easy and informal. The receptionist must have easy access to her doctor either in his office or by telephone. There should be no intimidation of the patients by the ancillary staff and the doctors should bend over backwards to avoid barriers with the staff who can so easily be overawed by the charisma of the profession.

As a medical student I assisted at a very difficult operation, and the surgeon completed the task with great skill and efficiency. Over a cup of coffee he asked, "Who is the most important person in the operating theatre?" Blinded by his technical skill, I plumped for the surgeon, but he told me I was wrong. The surgeon is a modest fellow I decided, and feeling any other suggestion was really beside the point I mentioned the theatre sister, and finally the anaesthetist. I am ashamed to say that I was quite mistaken in all my guesses and in my assessment of the surgeon, and the fact that the patient was the most important person in the theatre had never crossed my mind.

That the patient is also the most important person at a consultation is something we are inclined to forget. Without her we would all be out of work! If the atmosphere is right and the staff can correctly assess the patient's need, some who seek advice need go no further than the office desk. Such questions as the correct ages for immunization, or advice on the treatment of an invisible scratch may well be dealt with there and then.

An important and indeed essential virtue of all members of a doctor's team is discretion, and this applies to office staff every bit as much as to nursing services or the doctors themselves. Any receptionist or secretary is bound to have access to confidential information and this must never be revealed or talked about. One of the first instructions issued to a new recruit to the staff must be the importance of confidentiality. If the patients feel that they cannot trust the staff completely in this way, their contact with the receptionist is likely to be restrained and less cordial than it should be. It is because of the dangers of "leaks" that many doctors prefer to employ staff from outside the area practice. If this danger can be overcome, however, there are distinct advantages in having a local secretary. She knows what is going on in the community and can often be a great help because of this knowledge. "Mrs. Jones is coming to see you tonight. Her father was not a patient of ours, but he died suddenly of a heart attack last week." This information was, of course, quite invaluable and enhanced the usefulness of the consultation. On another occasion I was interested in two cousins who were suffering from a rare disease and my receptionist was able to name two other cousins with quite different names who were similar, thus creating a rare haul of an unusual syndrome.

This local knowledge of the community is very important. It would be ideal if the entire team of doctor, social workers, ancillary staff and also a dentist lived in the community in which they work. They should be visible at the local shops, at church if they are Christians, at many of the local functions. Only by living in the community in this way can they become an intimate part of it. Furthermore they should be approachable out of hours at their homes or on the telephone. Contrary to what many doctors think, people do not abuse the open line or the open house, and in a few minutes a word of advice or comfort at the right time can often do far more good than a whole hour later by appointment at the surgery. This sort of call is, in fact, a great rarity for people do try very hard not to trouble their doctor but, when one can help at such a time, it does a great deal of good. A depressed woman under treatment called to see me just as I was going in to a dinner party. She was in a state of very great agitation, but within ten minutes she felt a lot better and was profuse in her apologies for coming at the wrong time. I saw her at the surgery the next day and she was much more composed, and still apologetic for "spoiling my dinner." It is vital for the patients to feel they are important and that the doctor, nurse or the social worker does really care for them. Such a feeling gives them a security that they very rarely abuse.

7

The Share of the
Social Worker

MOST advances in social work have evolved from the inspiration of altruistic laymen. The Tukes of York were pioneers in the care of the mentally ill. Elizabeth Fry (1770-1845) was instrumental in bringing about prison reform, Florence Nightingale (1820-1910) volunteered to go to the Crimea, and the result was the foundation of the modern nursing services. The tendency is for voluntary agencies to pioneer various forms of social work and then gradually responsibility in each sphere is taken over by the State, often by the Local Authority backing the voluntary organization and using it as its agency. Since the passing of the Social Services Act of 1970 and the creation of a Local Authority Social Services Department as proposed in the Seebohm report, the local authorities have accepted full responsibility for most social problems. The name Social Services Department is perhaps a little unfortunate, as it is so easily confused with the Social Security Offices[1] dealing with problems of finance.

Before describing the various social services available, it is necessary to mention one or two agencies which are completely outside the jurisdiction of the Social Services Department. The probation service which is manned by trained and specialized social workers deals largely with adult crime and is controlled from the courts. Housing, employment and finance departments are not staffed by trained social workers, and are controlled by the District Councils, the Employment Exchange and the Department of Health and Social Security respectively. There is however

[1] The full title of this office is in fact the Supplementary Benefits Commission of the Department of Health and Social Security.

Depression: The Blue Plague

a close liaison between these agencies and the Department of Social Services.

Until 1970 there were several different departments providing social services and it was quite possible for a household in trouble to be visited by half a dozen or more social workers. A child care officer would call to look after the children, while a mental welfare officer was calling on the mother and someone else was helping the handicapped father, and there was little liaison between the various social workers. The Seebohm Report[2] produced a scheme to circumvent this problem. Its concept of social care was that there should be one door at which anyone could knock with any kind of problem. The result of this was to be that a social worker became family orientated, whereas previously she had been symptom orientated. The various problems to be tackled would include such diverse subjects as :

Marital problems and all problems of interpersonal relationships.
Difficulties with neighbours.
Mental health.
Problems with children.
Addictions of all kinds.
The aged.
The blind, the deaf and dumb, and handicapped people of all kinds.
Child offenders.
Homelessness.
Vagrancy.
Destitution.
One parent families.
Adoption.

Trained social workers would also act as a liaison between statutory and voluntary organizations in the community. Thus, with a broad basic training, the social case worker would deal with the family as a unit, trying to treat each individual as a whole person and not as a particular problem.

[2] Seebohm, F., *Local Authority Social Services Act* (H.M.S.O., 1970)

A woman of forty-two was widowed and was left with in-adequate finances to cope with a family of four. The eldest child was a very moody girl of eighteen and could not find work because she was epileptic. She was liable to periods of excitement in which she was quite dangerous; she did stupid things, but was not really aggressive. In one such mood she started some horse play with her twelve-year-old brother and broke his femur. She became mentally so upset, she had to be cared for for a few weeks in a mental hospital, and the unfortunate mother had to visit one child in a general hospital fifteen miles away, and the girl in the mental hospital eighteen miles away in another direction. Here was a whole series of problems, which included finding money for the mother to do her visiting, and someone to care for the children at home. The unhappy epileptic girl needed a good deal of support. The orthopaedic ward pressed the mother to call on the boy regularly as he was fretting, and later it was necessary to change the house round to help him when he came home on crutches.

In such a situation, one worker allocated to the household could be a great boon. Once the crisis had passed she could still be contacted for advice by the mother if trouble arose, and this was a great source of comfort. A widowed woman with an awkward family needs to have someone she can lean on without any feeling of obligation. Neighours and even relatives can get tired of helping and may have families of their own, and other responsibilities.

The district nurse and the health visitor work in conjunction with the family doctor, but the social case workers can often deal with the problem independently, and there is no need for medical intervention. The case worker dealing with the family may help them to accept or work through new problems. A woman was in trouble because her husband decided he was going to leave her and his family for a new woman he had picked up. A social worker who was dealing with their mongol child was able to intervene in her case work role. She was unable to produce a reconciliation but the wife was helped to accept the break up of her marriage. She was put in touch with a solicitor and supported through the ensuing legal process to obtain maintenance for herself and the children. There was no place in this case for any medical intervention. If, on the other hand, the social worker in a different situation found the husband was neglecting his family and not going to work, had queer ideas, and was behaving in a strange manner, a medical opinion on his mental state might be an urgent necessity, and here there would be a liaison with the family doctor.

Seebohm has certainly made it easier for the family in simplifying the pattern of social care, but it has made life much more difficult for the doctor. Instead of one mental welfare officer for his area, someone he has got to know as well as he knows his district nurse and health visitor, he now finds he has to co-operate with a dozen or more social workers. Each time he seeks help a new face appears, and this can be very disconcerting. However, the new arrangement has not been with us long, and the social worker and general practitioner partnership may well improve when we all get used to the new system. In any case, if the family has gained by the change over, we doctors should not complain.

So far I have described social workers dealing with families or individuals in trouble. There is also a great need for the community worker who will galvanize people to work in groups. The parents of mentally handicapped children can be helped in a number of ways if they can be brought together. Troubles seem less awful when they are shared by other parents, good ideas can be exchanged, and problems of mutual interest discussed. The talent for forming such a group, getting the participants thoroughly involved, and then leaving them to continue on their own is of great value to the community. There is such a need for this kind of work that social workers can never hope to carry the load on their own and must involve the community itself. In big towns, especially, creating a sense of community may have to be worked at and initiated by social workers in an endeavour to break down the loneliness and social isolation in which people can and do live in modern society, but the ultimate aim must be to involve the whole community to make the scheme self-supporting.

Societies and Community Colleges can do a lot to help in this direction, but such organizations only appeal to a minority, and while they offer an excellent service they are largely preaching to the converted. Community workers are trying to involve those who are not likely to involve themselves, sometimes by creating pressure groups to highlight a difficult problem. In doing so they do not always meet with the approval of the authorities. Housing schemes, some of which have involved squatting, may not have solved the problem, but they have brought to the attention of the public a difficult situation that many people would be only too willing to forget.

Alcoholism is another social evil which the community tends to sweep under the carpet, and almost nothing is being done to tackle it. The local psychiatric hospital which will accept the addict and dry him out, has little in the way of continued and radical treatment to offer and specialized addiction units are all too few. The best friend for any addict who really wishes to be rid of his problem is Alcoholics Anonymous, a completely voluntary organization. More of these pressure groups and forms of mutual aid associations are needed in the community, and the Social Services are seeking to foster this spirit. More will be said about this subject in the next chapter.

It is in the province of mental health that social workers come into closest contact with the blue plague. In the past the Mental Welfare Officers were adept in the art of taking disturbed patients to a psychiatric hospital and helping them over the initial difficulties. It is a very traumatic experience to be admitted to such a place, and moral support at this time is very welcome. I was always full of admiration for the skilful way in which the most reluctant patients were persuaded to go of their own free will, and here the decisive factor was often that the Mental Welfare Officer would take the patient in her own car. One of my colleagues got more than she bargained for when on one occasion she performed this act of charity, taking the patient to hospital literally weeping on her shoulder. Unfortunately it was not discovered until she reached the wards that her patient was heavily infested with head lice!

These workers were confident and competent because of their special training and wide experience but their parishes were far too large and they could not hope to do as much work as they would have liked in following up patients after mental illness. This is a difficult field into which social workers from the social services department are now to extend their range of experience. This kind of work raises a lot of fears and anxieties in people who did not initially choose to do it, and when it forms only a small part of their duties they have little opportunity to become accustomed to it and to develop expertise. It remains to be seen whether integration within the sphere of general social work will be possible or whether specialization will have to return. Whichever way it goes more time and more workers are needed for the proper care and supervision of the mentally sick.

Few patients relish the idea of being admitted to a psychiatric hospital, but if it becomes necessary it is a fact that has to be faced and the patient must never be cheated or deceived. She must be told exactly where she is going. If she is likely to object, cause a fuss or disappear, a great deal of time may be necessary to prepare her for this step, and ideally the process should not be hurried. She should be told she needs to have hospital treatment and this has been arranged. With tact and persuasion very few resist the idea for long. If real trouble is anticipated, more help should always be available than is likely to be needed. A show of force may impress the most deranged patient. I once had to send a paranoid schizophrenic into hospital, and he had a loaded shotgun ready to resist any form of compulsion. I did not enjoy paying a preliminary call to assess his mental state, as he was very offensive and had the gun ready on the sofa. His admission had to be organized like a military exercise, with a police sergeant and five police officers in two cars and an ambulance hidden round the corner. The Mental Welfare Officer and I kept in the background because we did not wish to upset him, as he hated us more than anyone else. We all stood by the cars while the sergeant and a single constable went straight to the house. He offered no resistance in the face of such a show of force, only asking to travel in a police car. Such occasions are rare and admission to psychiatric hospital is usually managed with compassion and care.

Return to the community can be almost as difficult for the patient and some form of follow up is essential. I personally make a point of visiting patients discharged from a psychiatric ward. I like to make them welcome into the community, and I want to know just how they feel, whether they have really recovered, and whether they feel that the treatment was worthwhile. Complaints against their care in a psychiatric hospital are now very rare. Often the patient smiles in an embarrassed way, and makes light of her illness. She cannot imagine why she was so stupid as to have behaved as she did. Memory of the admission is usually very clear in the patient's mind. One woman who had slapped my face on such an occasion expected me to bear her malice for her behaviour, and was relieved to see that this was not the case.

Provided there has been no deception about the admission, I have never known any lasting resentment on the part of the patient. At this first visit to the home, I try to keep her feet on the ground. It is important not to let the patient get away with a smiling pretence that it has all been something of a mistake. I emphasize that they have recovered from an *illness*, an illness as real as boils or pneumonia, which like those illnesses is treatable. Having discussed the past briefly in this way, I direct their attention to the future. What is the patient going to do now? How soon can she get back to work? And so on. Recovery is not complete until the patient is back at work and fully employed. This may be at a local factory, or running a home with toddlers crawling round the kitchen floor.

Usually I make only one visit and thereafter the patient is given an appointment at the surgery, since it is good for the invalid to get out and to mix with people again. Social workers either from the hospital or from the community are often involved in this kind of work. The patient while in hospital should be prepared for her discharge and the relatives at home should be visited and advised about the homecoming since there may well be questions to be answered or problems to be solved. Finally, once the patient is at home, steps must be taken to ensure rehabilitation goes as smoothly as possible, with a return to full employment at an early date if this can be achieved.

Once the recovery is complete, there may be nothing further for the social worker to do, but if there are residual symptoms, or the patient is still under treatment, then collaboration with the family doctor may be necessary. For a time most discharged patients attend a psychiatric out-patient department, but if the family doctor is prepared to accept full responsibility for the patient, and there is a lot to be said for this, links with the psychiatric unit may well be broken at an early stage.

If this kind of routine is not followed, the discharge of a patient into the community may have disastrous results. A poor old woman hermit of seventy-five lived alone in penury. Up to the time when I saw her she had never had a fire in the hearth or any heating since her husband had died eight years before. She told me she found the heat from the electric light bulb adequate! She was cared for by two married nieces who took it in turns to take her a dinner and see she had food. Suddenly she turned against these women and accused them of stealing her money. The doors were bolted and barred and no one was admitted. After two days of unavailing attempts at persuasion, the police were asked to force an entry, which they did with difficulty. Inside I found the woman, a paranoid eccentric, undernourished and in need of care, and I had her admitted to a psychiatric hospital. Six weeks later she was sent home. No one came to see where she was going to live or who was going to look after her, or if indeed she was prepared to let people into her house. Her stay in the well heated hospital ward had lowered her resistance to cold, and on her return to her own home she contracted pneumonia and died. It was clearly wrong to discharge her without adequate preparation initiated by the hospital staff, and executed by the family with the aid of a social worker.

Many patients discharged from hospital are soon standing on their own feet and need no further help or supervision. This is the ideal recovery at which all social workers should aim.

Greaves[3] is strongly in favour of nurses from the mental hospitals carrying out after care. This should be very useful in certain cases, especially if the necessary medication could be given at the same time, but it seems a bit extravagant in nurse time and petrol, since psychiatric hospitals often have a catchment area with a radius of thirty miles. In stressing as she does in her paper the need for after care, Miss Greaves is right, but my own feeling is that this should in most cases be provided by the social services or general practice services working on the spot. If this is to be done adequately we will need many more trained social workers.

It has already been shown that there are recurrent episodes of depression in about eighty per cent of patients. It is not very encouraging to draw a convalescent patient's attention to this possibility, and when asked if another attack is likely, I say no one can tell, but there is a good chance this may be the only attack, and I point out that it is, in any case, a treatable illness. If, however, the patient has recovered from her fourth or fifth episode, another attack is likely, and I warn the next of kin rather than the patient, and ask the husband to insist on an early consultation if ever he has cause to worry again.

There are, alas, chronic cases. These have already been described, and with such problems the family need a good deal of moral support over perhaps many years. Here the social worker allocated to the family can be of great value. I can think of a man who became very depressed in 1947. He was only forty years old at the time. He had every form of treatment available, culminating in leucotomy, but nothing helped him and he has never worked since. He and his wife had a family of five sons, two of whom developed a severe congenital ataxia and they too have been unemployed for many years. The mainstay of the family was the wife, who not only coped well with a very difficult family, but was always ready to help anyone else in trouble in the street. This family unit have managed very well thanks to the very exceptional character of the wife, but in similar circumstances a family might well have been unable to cope with the many crises

[3] Greaves, G. M. (1972). *British Hospital Journal and Social Service Review*, October, 7.

that are bound to occur, without the help of long term social work support.

Working in an area such as ours, where mental health is viewed as an essential part of general practice, there must be a good deal of liaison with the family doctor. In the past I certainly found myself leaning very heavily on the mental welfare officer for help and support and advice. She was never called upon as much in the practice as the nurses or the health visitor, but she was just as important, and the lines of communication just as close. This is very important from every angle. Some patients in this sphere are rather liable to play one party off against another, and unless the social worker and doctor keep in close touch, they can be led right up the garden path by this type of patient. This is particularly important to remember at this changing period in the social services. General practitioners find themselves in contact with many new social workers in this field and social workers are in touch with many general practitioners; it is an area that generates considerable alarm and uncertainty in some people and there is often undoubtedly a lack of confidence between the two disciplines. It is easy for further damaging alienation to occur if it is not thoroughly appreciated on both sides that what the disturbed patient reports of the other must be suspect and that good direct lines of communication must be established. There are, of course, doctors who are just not interested in this kind of problem, and with such practices the social services or the psychiatric hospital staff will have far more to do in following up and supporting the patient. It is an important job and someone must do it if the best results for the patient are to be achieved.

8

The Responsibility of
the Community

I WAS in the middle of a surgery, when I received an emergency call to a road accident nearby. I told my patient to wait, thinking that I would soon be back, but how wrong I was. On the road a quarter of a mile from the surgery I found Jimmy lying in a pool of blood, deeply unconscious, bleeding from both ears and from his nose and his scalp which was badly lacerated. I wrapped an emergency pack bandage round his head, and then, to my relief, the ambulance arrived, but, as it was accompanied by only the driver, I decided to go with the boy to hospital. We covered the fifteen miles in about twenty minutes which was pretty good going, but I wondered if Jimmy would last out until we got there. He was alive on arrival and was whisked straight into the theatre. He was in the intensive care unit for two weeks, but he died in the end, the only child of middle aged parents who had no chance of having further children of their own.

Jimmy's parents lived in a new housing estate, and most of the residents were strangers to each other and to the village. This devastating tragedy had a remarkable effect. Everyone on the estate rallied to do what they could to comfort the parents, and to help in any way possible. Money was raised so that a cup could be bought to commemorate Jimmy in a local sports event. The British Legion had a collection and money was raised to buy some needed item for the intensive care unit. One of the local clergy saw that Jimmy's toys were taken to a needy orphanage, and some of the folk on the estate helped to rearrange and redecorate the house. This activity and goodwill offered immeasurable help to the grieving parents, and it certainly sustained them through their crisis. It also was of great value to the estate itself: the people became more friendly and mixed in a way they had not done before.

All this action was spontaneous, and very useful. People do rally in an emergency: but we do not want emergencies of this kind to bring new communities to life. To be of lasting value the surge of goodwill must in some way be sustained, and without some sort of planned effort this is unlikely to happen. This is why there is a desperate need for community-orientated organizations.

In the past this side of life was catered for by the Church. People who moved to a new place automatically went to the nearest church. Not only were there services to attend on high days and holy days, but there were collateral organizations, like the Mothers' Union, the various youth organizations, choirs and dramatic societies for people with special talents. More philanthropic people could support missionary efforts or charitable institutions. The Church's influence was widespread and could provide a full and satisfying social life.

Today, when so few people go to church, the influence of religious bodies is correspondingly reduced. People moving to a new area rarely feel there is an organization to which they belong by right and in which they will find social satisfaction. Instead they tend to seek solace at pubs and clubs or the local bingo hall, and though the more sociable of them will find cheerful companionship in this way these groups are no substitute for an organization which demands a service from its members, and binds them together by common effort. The less sociable newcomers often fall back on patent medicines and tranquillizers to mask the loneliness and emptiness of their days.

The impact of the blue plague has not gone entirely unnoticed by churchmen. In the early fifties Chad Varah, a London priest, founded the Samaritans. He had been impressed by the number of suicides in Greater London and wondered if anything could be done to help these depressed people, and all the victims of the blue plague, before it was too late. He started his work in the vestry of St. Stephen's, Walbrook. He asked for volunteers to man a telephone day and night, and he collected a band of experts who were prepared to turn out at all hours to help and comfort those in dire distress. He found counsellors who were prepared to advise the less urgent cases about their problems, and he was able to channel his clients to the most appropriate existing services. I have already suggested that many depressed people are very reluctant to seek the help of their own doctors. Some failed to do so in the past because they had felt their doctor was quite unsympathetic towards them and their problems. By approaching the Samaritans, the sick person was assured of a sympathetic ear, and in any case it is sometimes easier to talk to a stranger than the family physician. This was very clearly demonstrated by one of my own patients whom I had helped before. As the clouds of depression descended a second time, she could not bring herself to seek my help again but grew more and more desperate, and in the end telephoned the Samaritans in our nearby town. They, of course, referred her back to me, not without some amusement, as they know my sympathy and concern for such cases. Because it was designed to meet such a genuine need the Samaritan movement spread out rapidly from London, so that the emergency telephone number can be found in heavy print in the telephone directory of every big city. Depressed persons can ring up at any hour, and their problem will be dealt with. Not only has the movement helped many depressed and confused people, but it has built up a community of volunteers who are prepared to spend leisure hours manning the telephone, or turning out at an inconvenient time to counsel or console some person in distress. There are many thousands of volunteers in the organization. Jimmy's death on the road produced a surge of goodwill on a new housing estate. Chad Varah's inspiration has gone much further. He has initiated a viable service run by the community for the community. We need far more of his kind of pressure group for other social problems.

There are, of course, in Western society many excellent philanthropic societies or organizations which do an immense amount of good, in providing interest and companionship for their members and they can do a fine job in the community in all sorts of ways. Money may be raised to provide a van for Meals on Wheels

so that more old people may be better fed, poor families provided
with holidays and countless other good works. Their limitation
as useful social units is that they can only draw in people who
enjoy that kind of activity, and who are ready to come forward
and offer to help. They can only serve those sections of society
which have made their needs known : it is difficult to get at the
masses who most need help but have no idea where to start finding a solution to their problems. Providing facilities is only half
the battle, for only a proportion of people are able to make use of
their opportunities. We have, for instance, an excellent club for
old people in our area. They have weekly meetings with tea and
a bun. Lectures at the community college are arranged, outings
in the summer, parties and shows in the winter, and cheap holidays are organized in the off-peak season. This well run service
caters for about two hundred pensioners in the village, but here
lies the problem : ' there must be two or three times that number
who do not take advantage of the facilities. There are many
causes such as lack of transport, illness, disability and so on, but
the main cause is a basic inertia which occurs in all of us but is
more evident in old people. They cannot be bothered to turn
out and seem unable to help themselves. This inability to make
the necessary effort to mix with others and achieve a fuller life is
common at all ages but most common in old age, where it becomes even more obviously a positive danger to health.

Man is a social animal, he needs the company of his own
kind, although there is a limit to the number of intimate friends
one can have and entertain. It has been suggested that few can
tolerate a close circle of more than fifteen to twenty persons, although one can of course have many more than this number of
acquaintances. This numerical limitation of close friends is possibly a throwback to the old tribal structure, and modern man
at heart still yearns for the cosy intimacy of the small group.
Without human contacts he is in a very vulnerable situation. Very
few of us can live as hermits and if we try to do so we may very
soon find ourselves in trouble. A lone yachtsman told me how,
after a few days, he found himself prone to vivid hallucinations.

If one is compelled to live alone, it takes a good deal of self discipline even to maintain a decent standard of hygiene. If old people living alone are observed, all too often one can see a gradual social, physical and mental deterioration. Under such circumstances the diet tends to consist of far too much starch and to be deficient in protein and vitamins. All too readily, bread and jam becomes the staple diet. It suits the purse, and such meals need no preparation. Bathing becomes a burden, so the habit is dropped. Slowly but surely the house becomes as dirty and unkempt as its occupier. The old person nods off at odd times during the day, and then cannot sleep at night. If because of this she can secure sleeping tablets from her doctor she readily becomes addicted. Drugged sleep is a pleasant escape from the monotony of life, and she tends to increase the dose, and to take the tablets earlier each night. Finally she is going to bed at 6.00 p.m., and by 2.00 a.m. is making cups of tea and complains more than ever of being unable to sleep.

The solution to the problem of loneliness in old age depends upon a number of factors. First, even in old age, people have a responsibility towards themselves, although with advancing age it becomes increasingly difficult to sustain. Secondly there is the family unit. Most of us need a good deal of care and stimulation from our own kith and kin. Thirdly the community itself can do a great deal to help by schemes which are beyond the powers or the purse of the ordinary citizen. The spirit of altruism is peculiar to the human race, but it tends to be a recessive characteristic. It needs to be encouraged if it is to flourish, and its very existence in philanthropic bodies is a sign of great cultural advancement.

Some fortunate people are able to make the best of things, and are never sorry for themselves. They are cheerful people and have the knack of getting the best out of everyone. But such a capacity for happiness is a rare gift, few of us have it, and most old people have to depend on others to keep them cared for and happy. Contentment in old age depends on a number of factors. Reasonable health is welcome, but that alone will not bring happiness. The old person needs a fair amount of company, but at the same time be able to get away on her own for a rest or a sleep. If she can do things with her hands, work on embroidery, knit squares and make blankets, or enjoy a game of cards, all these things help. To be able to read is a great boon that few in our local community enjoy. Periodic company, admiration, and independence are necessary. This can be achieved in the home of her children but it is not easy.

Today a tremendous amount of thought is being put into accommodation for the elderly that will meet these requirements. Regrettably some "homes" are still being built that provide no outlet for independence, individuality or stimulus and we still have the sad sight of groups of old people sitting idle, sad and socially neglected, although their surroundings have been changed from those of squalor to great comfort. The creation of flatlets by the community or some other kind of sheltered but independent accommodation by various groups of philanthropists are some of the best ways in which the community is helping old people today. Obviously this kind of place cannot provide nursing through a long illness, but with the help of neighbours and the family, it is surprising what can be done. Even very disabled and sometimes mentally frail old people can be tolerated and maintained in society as respectable independent citizens.

These old people do, however, need help and supervision. The relatives, social workers and the wardens need to be on the lookout for troubles which often a little extra help can solve. One highly intelligent old woman in a local flatlet was crippled with rheumatism, and found it very difficult to get to the toilet in time. As a result her personal hygiene left much to be desired and, while she washed her own underclothes as best she could, she was fighting a losing battle. She began to smell, and soon her room stank. She felt depressed, humiliated and completely unable to solve her problem. A committee member, realizing her difficulties, approached her family about it. A kindly woman was employed to clean the room each day and to attend to the laundry. A nurse called to bath the old woman, and the patient was provided with a commode in her room, so that she no longer had to struggle to the toilet every time. The daily woman emptied the commode. In no time the smells had gone, and the old person was relieved of her sense of impotent shame which was making

124

it impossible for her to mix with her friends and neighbours.

Few are blessed with a perennially good nature and most people enjoy a good grumble which, if received sympathetically, makes them feel better. Old people in sheltered accommodation are no exception : they find things to grumble about. The flat is too hot or too cold, or a neighbour is too noisy, the warden too quiet. They can tell their family all about it when they call, and feel better, especially if appropriate noises of agreement are made. How different it is for the old person who lives with her family. She likes to grouse too, and she may have plenty to complain about. If she does so to the family her comments at best are met with indifference, at worst with some angry retort. To grumble to friends about the family smacks disloyalty, and so the old person loses a useful safety valve.

There is no room for complacency about this problem, and much remains to be done. There are still many old folk who battle on in isolation who refuse to help themselves by joining clubs organized for their benefit, and some of these people have no relatives to keep popping in to cheer them up and keep them in touch with the outside world. These people can be given cards or lamps to put in the window if they need help, but if they fall, for instance, and break a leg, they cannot reach the card or the window. Street wardens or a rota of senior scouts and guides who will call *each day* to do small jobs and see all is well, seem to be the best answer to this difficult problem, but in most places such ideas are just pipe dreams. It is only after the milk bottles have piled up unused that the house is broken into to find the lonely corpse has been dead for days, and the community is shocked for a while by the realization of its neglect.

A good deal of time has been spent in discussing the responsibility of the community for the elderly, but each age group has its problems, many of which are a challenge to the community. Until recently it was assumed that the very young were adequately catered for in their homes and schools. In an affluent society they are no longer starved and ragged, and primary education in particular has been transformed to provide interest and stimulus. Today there is mounting anxiety about the pre-school period and a growing demand for nursery schools to supplement parental care at an even earlier age. "Operation Head Start" in America has been created to attempt to cope with the inequality of opportunity in the pre-school group. In the process of growing up the first overt trouble spot comes with the teenagers who have grown too big for the nest, but have not developed to the point where they have their own niche in society. The majority are passive creatures and accept the *status quo*. If a girl, her ideal in life is to find a boy friend, get married and live in the house next door to mum. If a boy, he gets a job, lives at home and pays his board. He likes a drink at the weekends and may well be a staunch supporter of the football team, but he is content with a pretty humdrum existence. A minority of people get bored with life and yearn for adventure and excitement.

The human male is far more aggressive than the female, and nowhere is this sex difference better demonstrated than in the prison population of England and Wales. In round figures there are some forty thousand male inmates and only nine hundred women. The aggression, the longing for excitement, can be canalized into useful and socially accepted channels. Some find an outlet for this in fellwalking, potholing, games of all sorts, and outward bound groups. These occupations are excellent. They produce self reliance, healthy comradeship, and in an emergency the strong urge to risk life and limb to help others in trouble. Other young people become definitely antisocial, with muggers, football hooligans, and hell's angels as outstanding examples. They seek out violence and enjoy fighting. They get satisfaction in moving about in gangs looking for trouble and will take on allcomers—a rival group, the police, or any innocent bystander. The more ruthless and violent the character, the more he is admired by the group.

A third category of the young swing completely away from violence which they abhor. They drift about philosophizing, criticizing the way the world ticks in Western society, but they have no active or positive suggestions to make, and seem to feel the world owes them a living. They experiment with alcohol, drugs, sex, yoga and religions of all kinds. They sleep rough, and hitch hike round the world with the wealthy car owners they despise, seeking peace and contentment. India and its religion is often their Mecca. In spite of their claims to unworldliness, tolerance and universal love, they seem uncertain of themselves and unhappy at heart, unlikely to help society forward into a better stage or to help to solve its problems.

Prince Philip, in his inaugural address as President to the Royal College of General Practitioners in 1972, suggested that symptoms of ill health in the community were becoming increasingly obvious in petty crime and violence. The old principle of finding the guilty and meting out punishment was not enough, was not in fact the answer. Society had to look deeper to find the causes of these social ills. There is certainly much to be done. We have as yet no remedy for the ills of these antisocial or inadequate young people. They are not interested in joining the youth clubs and venture scouts that help others so much, and if they transgress the law neither reformatories nor prison provide an effective answer. However, in time a surprising number of these wild or anxious young people do settle down and marry, and all their energy is put into creating a home. On the television screen they see how the other half lives, and this they want to emulate.

There are always a few problem families who live in great squalor but they form only a small minority, and some would say they suffer from an incurable social disease. In a rural community such as ours, I have seen a few children from such homes do far better than their parents, adopting much higher standards on leaving home. The majority, however, are overwhelmed by their hopeless environment and tend to stay in the same slovenly rut they have always known. The care for such families is one of the greatest problems for social workers, and they extort from the community far more help and attention than the average citizen, with very small return.

There is one sphere in which our community does less for the individual today than it did in the past, and this is in handling situations of death and mourning. Gorer[1] has said that death

[1] Gorer, G., *Death, Grief and Mourning in Contemporary Britain* (Cresset Press, 1965).

has replaced sex as the most taboo subject in modern society. Fifty years ago death was commonplace in every family. A baby weighing less than five pounds at birth had scant hope of survival. Diphtheria and scarlet fever killed many young children, and pneumonia had earned the title of "Captain of the men of Death." Pulmonary tuberculosis, the White Plague, carried off many young people and others in the prime of life. Today, apart from road accidents, death among the young is rare. The loss of parents is in the natural order of events and is generally accepted without too much trouble, but the loss of a spouse or a child is a far more difficult problem.

From the dawn of history the three major events in life have been birth, marriage, and death, and to meet such situations, elaborate rituals were evolved. Birth and marriage were joyful occasions and are therefore not a part of our problem, but all the complex funeral rites provided a framework of support in a very difficult time and went a long way to comfort the mourners. Well established rituals helped a widow, for instance, and she knew that the family would rally round her and take all responsibilities off her shoulders. She was encouraged to talk about what happened, and her morale was raised by repeated praises for the deceased husband. Eulogies for the dead were not confined to words. The coffin had to be lined, festal garbs donned, floral tribues donated, and no matter how ghoulish the situation, those who viewed the body were all agreed he looked "lovely and so peaceful." The funeral was of necessity a harrowing experience, which was countered by the feast which followed. Friends and relatives came from far and wide, food was eaten, beer or wine consumed, a confrontation of many people who rarely met, but were pleased to see each other again, took place. In this way tensions were eased, and the greater family departed to leave the widow in the care of children or siblings.

In the past the ritual continued for many weeks. Widow's weeds were the order of the day, or a black arm band for those who could not afford full mourning. The wealthy wrote letters on paper with a black border, matched by similar envelopes. All social activities were halted for a prescribed time, and the entire family went to church where front pews were reserved for them. Everyone knew what to expect and how to behave, and provision was made for tears and expressions of grief. In those days bereaved parents could take comfort in the fact that this was the lot of most families, they were not alone in their sorrow. The rituals meant they knew what to do and what was expected of them and most people had experience of death before they grew up.

Things are different today for a number of reasons. While widowhood is just as common, deaths in childhood are now rare. Many young adults have no knowledge of how to cope with death and their society provides no rules or customs for their guidance. What can happen today is illustrated by the death of a young woman in a motor accident. Her fiancé was not involved in the crash. He wore no black armband, so that unless people had read or heard of the accident, they did not realize he was a mourner. If they did know, what were they to do? Should they ask him out for a meal, could they invite him to a dance? In the absence of the formalities of yesterday, these decisions can be very difficult both for the man himself and his friends.

Fortunately youth has great resilience and most young people get over these tragedies, but it would be better if people understood more fully the process of mourning. Confronted with death the usual first reaction is one of tears. This is nature's way of relieving tensions and it is to be encouraged. It is surprising how often the response of a well meaning relative is to say "Don't cry," when tears can be so helpful. It is also a great pity that, in our Anglo-Saxon society, it is considered unmanly for the male to cry, thereby adding to the strain of the male mourners who, to comply with custom, have to hold back their tears.

Sometimes the immediate reaction is one of anger against the doctor, the hospital or the self. I remember being present at the deathbed of a man I much admired. I was relieved to be there when he actually died, as I felt his widow would need a good deal of support. Her first reaction was one of violent anger directed against me, which had to be accepted as a symptom of stress until the mood passed and she could accept my help.

Sometimes there is an attitude of complete unbelief. The woman keeps saying "He is not dead is he?" and just cannot accept what has happened. Another reaction is one of numbness or blunting of consciousness in which the bereaved person behaves as if nothing has happened. Sometimes there is a kind of false complacency about the event. A woman who lost her four-week-old baby from an acute infection told me she was glad he had died before she had learned to love him fully. Once the first reaction is over, there is a period of intermittent distress which occurs in waves. The mourner tends to be apathetic and depressed and often feels that life is futile. At times she feels as if her husband is back again, he is standing just behind her, or she looks at the window expecting him to peer through at her, or she finds herself going upstairs to look for him. Sleep is often a problem, the appetite diminishes, and it may be very difficult to concentrate or do things.

No one knows just how long mourning should last, and obviously there are individual variations. It is useful to have some figures in mind. It has been suggested that the mourner should be able to cope with normal work after two weeks and that the sense of loss has become tolerable by six months[2] although the whole twelve months are very traumatic as anniversaries come and go. The average widow, of course, still misses her husband, but she becomes adjusted to the situation. There will for a long time still be surges of yearning and depression on anniversaries, or occasions when she is suddenly reminded about her husband. Bowen[3], writing on this subject, has suggested that on the death of a spouse, the survivor is at the same time deprived of the one person to whom she can talk freely about all her troubles. In such a situation the bereaved person is in great need of a substitute in the form of a skilled and sympathetic listener. This may well be a minister of religion, the family doctor, a social

[2] Murray-Parkes, C., *British Journal of Medical Psychology*, 38.1.
[3] Bowen, A. (1973). *The Practitioner*, **210,** 127.

worker, or a close friend who is able to impart the necessary comfort.

Death may come suddenly or unexpectedly, or it may be the termination of a long and painful illness. In either case the family unit has a price to pay in suffering. Sudden death is a nice way out for the victim, but a severe shock for the relatives, and adjustment to the new situation can be very difficult. On the other hand, if the sick person lingers in pain and discomfort, so that the family are relieved when the struggle is over, the suffering is largely borne by the sick person. After such an illness it is usually easier for the family to come to terms with the new situation. Whether death comes quickly or slowly, at such a time the family is usually in need of a good deal of support. In this field Margaret Torrie has tried to do for the widow what Chad Varah has done for the depressed. She has launched an organization called Cruse which sets out to help and advise widows. Her book for such women[4] is a comprehensive volume on the subject of women living alone. All social workers should know about it and it is an excellent present for any widowed relative. Branches of Cruse are not as widespread as they should be yet, but up and down the country there are many societies for single people which serve a very useful purpose.

There are so many sections of society which need help, and this can only be achieved by action and pressure from within the community itself. There are not enough resources or social workers to do everything, and self help by the community is essential if these problems are to be tackled. Except in the stress of some crisis, individuals are reluctant to interfere or suggest help, preferring to believe it is not their business or their problem. This was splendidly illustrated by an experiment of Professor Neil Kessel.[5] He asked a pretty young actress to visit six chemists shops within a mile of each other in Edinburgh. The girl sobbed and cried and looked a picture of distress, and at each shop she asked for two hundred aspirins. As Kessel pointed out there could be no economic motive for buying so many tablets as the

[4] Torrie, M., *Begin Again* (Dent, 1970).
[5] Kessel, N. (1965). *British Medical Journal*, **2,** 1138.

largest bottle on sale contains only one hundred tablets. Nowhere was she refused her request. The nearest approach to compassion was shown by one chemist who asked her "if she was all right" and advised her to go home and get a cup of tea. She received many curious glances, but no offer of help, no one showed any desire to inquire why she was in such a state, or what she might be going to do, and this lack of interest was not only from her fellow customers or the man in the street, but from responsible persons who knew the dangers of aspirins.

With this spirit of inertia in the community, it is not surprising to find it difficult to establish permanent welfare groups as viable propositions. Perhaps it is surprising to find there are so many. The Red Cross Society and Alcoholics Anonymous have already been mentioned. Unmarried mothers in some parts have organized their own groups such as "Mothers in Action" or "The Ginger Bread Group." The parents of disabled or mentally handicapped children find they are helped by getting together and creating their own clubs. There are many of these organizations already in the community but many more are needed. They must grow from within, founded on common interests and needs, led by one of their own members with initiative and drive but they must be supported and maintained and valued by the community as a whole. With proper support they can do a tremendous amount to dispel despair and to discharge to some extent the community's responsibility to its handicapped members, and combat the blue plague at vulnerable points.

9

Summing up

MANY people are asking if people today are more neurotic anxious or depressed than were our forebears. The plain answer is that we do not know with certainty, for there are no statistics to show how many people were ill in this kind of way two hundred years ago. The actual patterns of illness have not changed and we can find all the various types portrayed in the literature of byegone days. The impression is that mental illness is on the increase. Mills[1] suggested that the fantastic increase in self-poisoning indicated an increase in depression which was in turn a symptom of stress induced by the steady rise of population pressure. Bailey, a journalist, wrote[2] that mental illhealth has practically reached epidemic proportions when every child born in Britain is ten times more likely to be admitted to a mental hospital than to a University. He gave no figures, and indeed significantly accurate statistics are hard to come by. Shepherd[3] listed a series of general practice surveys and the figures for mental troubles varied from four per cent to sixty-five per cent of the practice populations. With a difference of this magnitude it is obvious that the definition of psychoneurotic varies from doctor to doctor, since the actual prevalence could not vary in the community to that extent.

If it is difficult to compare the prevalence of mental illness in its broadest sense from one British practice to another, how much more complicated it becomes to compare the figures from country to country or indeed from one century to the next. The suicide

[1] Mills, I. (1972). *Steroids in Modern Medicine, Syntex Pharmaceuticals*, March, p. 3.
[2] Bailey, A. (1972), Harpers Magazine, March, p. 94.
[3] Shepherd, M., Cooper, B., Brown, A. C. and Kalton, G. W., *Psychiatric Illness in General Practice* (Blackwell, 1966).

rate is one guide but, as has already been shown, this is a very inaccurate measure. People tend to be guided more by impressions than hard facts and figures, and impressions can be wrong. Do the starving millions of India suffer as much from neuroses as do the affluent Western peoples? The general impression is that neurosis tends to be more a luxury for leisured wealthy communities. Certainly few, if any, of the poor in India can afford to consult a doctor but it does seem as if people in real trouble have not the time nor the energy to be neurotic. Physical illness even in Western society can rapidly displace a neurosis. I remember a man full of sexual obsessions who contracted pneumonia. While physically ill, his mental problems receded, and he told me his pneumonia was far easier to bear than his neurosis. Working in rural Africa, I formed the impression that while psychoses occurred among the black people as among the whites, neuroses were far less in evidence. The weakness in this deduction was that there was no means of knowing how many of those with neurotic types of illness repaired to the witch doctor who understood their culture and background. In any case the question as to whether or not there is more psychoneurotic illness today than at the beginning of the century or in other parts of the world is purely academic. There is quite enough in the community to give rise to concern. The big problem is what can be done to help such people.

An unexpected development in the last thirty years is that mental illnesses such as endogenous depression or schizophrenia are in fact easier to treat than anxiety and the neurotic syndromes. The psychoses are often due to a biochemical upset, and most cases of endogenous depression make a good response to anti-depressant drugs. This type of illness does necessitate medical intervention, and all persons who may be suffering from a severe mental illness should be referred to a doctor. The term mental illness does not imply the patient "is going mad." There is often very little wrong except a minor chemical imbalance which can easily be rectified.

If the patient is suffering from anxiety or stress, there are no drugs of comparable value to ease or correct the situation. By far the most important treatment is psychotherapy in some form, and this is not the sacred preserve of the doctor. It can be carried out by trained social workers, clergy, teachers, or marriage guidance counsellors, but to perform effective work in this field does demand a lengthy period of training. No one can perform useful psychotherapy by the light of nature, and amateurs in this field can find themselves in great trouble. The local vicar who spends too much time comforting a middle aged widow may suddenly find himself far more emotionally entangled than he realized was possible. The trained therapist is always a jump or two ahead of his patient. He realizes that the woman is becoming sexually attached to him before she realizes this herself, and he is on his guard against becoming too involved.

Medawar[4] suggested that any successful form of psychotherapy had certain clearly defined characteristics.

1. There is the assurance of a regular sympathetic hearing.
2. There is the feeling that someone is taking his condition seriously.
3. The patient discovers there are others in the same predicament.
4. There is comfort in learning that the condition is explicable.

To this list I would add a fifth factor, and that is the intimate bond which is forged between the patient and the therapist. It has names such as "good bedside manner," "a good rapport" or "a positive transference." Apart from being a skilled advisor, the therapist can act as a kind of catalyst; without saying much, without giving advice, he can help the patient to understand his problem more clearly, and perhaps come to terms with it. There is something gratifying, mysterious and unique about confidential two way meetings. It is one of the great bonds in married life, where everything and anything is discussed by husband and wife. Hopes and fears are shared. All decisions in life great or small are discussed. There are little communications between the two all the time, most often by speech but sometimes by way of a look, a smile, a wink, or a kick under the table. Little jokes are

4 Medawar, P. B., *The Art of the Soluble* (Methuen, 1968).

shared which would be completely humourless in other company. It is something in the intimate exchange rather than its content that gives both partners comfort and support. The Church, by way of the confessional, made very good use of this powerful weapon. By confession and absolution, a great deal of the sting could be taken out of a guilty conscience and the bond linking people with their confessor, as someone with whom they are completely honest and open, is in itself helpful and therapeutic.

In the field of medicine the situation has been beautifully described by the late Sir James Spence who was a great teacher, clinician and inspiration to generations of medical students. "The real work of a doctor is not an affair of health centres, or public clinics, or operating theatres, or laboratories or hospital beds. Techniques have their place in medicine, but they are not medicine. The essential unit of medical practice is the occasion when, in the intimacy of the consulting room or the sick room, a person who is ill, or believes himself to be ill, seeks the advice of a doctor whom he trusts. This is a consultation and all else in the practice of medicine derives from it."[5] The same sort of thing applies to any situation where a sick person or one who believes himself to be sick consults a trained social worker. In some cases the patient can be helped merely by listening. In other cases listening must be augmented by explanation or interpretation, and some may need to be referred to the family doctor or to a consultant.

The principles suggested by Medawar are well worth discussing in greater detail. Regular sessions are usually necessary, but with an experienced therapist five, ten, certainly not more than twenty minutes are enough for the majority of patients and six such interviews are usually adequate. If the patient has not improved after that time, further sessions are unlikely to bring about recovery, but short supportive interviews may be necessary to maintain the patient. There are people who need to lean on somebody, often for a few weeks only, sometimes for a few months, occasionally indefinitely. One such chronic patient had a good deal of insight into her problems, but she was always an

[5] Spence, J. C., *The Purpose and Practice of Medicine* (Blackwell, 1960).

anxious, nervous type of person. She leaned for support on her mother whom she saw every day in life. She admitted she had a greater affinity for her than for her husband. When her mother suddenly died she was plunged into a state of great agitation and depression, and as her doctor I had to supply the support, weekly for many months. She never took up much of my time, but she had to feel there was someone to whom she could turn in her distress. After a very long time of supportive treatment she managed to stand on her own feet, and now I rarely see her.

Regular sessions, freely offered and accepted are much more satisfying than a grudging two minutes during which a prescription for a vast number of tranquillizers is completed. In this time nothing useful is done and both doctor and patient are wasting energy in hating each other. The doctor says to himself that here is another stupid time consuming neurotic, and he wishes she would go somewhere else. The patient feels that the doctor disapproves of her and her illness, and she is angry because she dares not ask the questions that are bothering her and making recovery impossible. Regular short sessions during which the patient can talk or ask questions are far less traumatic and can, in the long run, prove to have helped the patient to regain confidence in herself.

This leads on, of course, to the second of Medawar's principles which was that the patient must feel that her problem is being taken seriously. With sick people like this there is no place for sarcasm or slick answers. Above all the patient must not be made, in any way, to lose face. The average psychoneurotic feels pretty inferior and lacking in confidence, and the whole object of treatment is to get the patient back to a situation where she has confidence and is master of her own fate. This is rarely, if ever, effected by a snub. The psychoneurotic does tend to feel she is alone with her worries, and to learn there are other people like her, and that she has a legitimate claim on the doctor's or the social worker's time comes as quite a relief.

Any intelligent person deserves, if he so requires, an explanation of what has gone wrong, how his whole life situation is affecting him, and what the social worker or the doctor is hoping to do for him. An explanation can be very consoling. Medawar boldly adds that success does not necessarily depend on the explanation being the right one as long as it is reasonable and acceptable to the patient. This suggestion may shock the purist but as no one, even a therapist, is omniscient, it is a comforting conception. A woman came to see me about sexual incompatibility with her husband. I spent many sessions over several weeks with her. One morning she arrived and told me she felt completely recovered and would not need my help any more. She had reached her thirty-seventh birthday and the clouds had suddenly lifted. She realized she had been obsessed by a fear of dying in her thirty-sixth year as her mother had done, although she had never faced or revealed this fact. In some way discussing her other problems had helped her over an awkward period of her life. False explanations of her troubles and the comfort of having a sympathetic listening had, as it were, kept her going until time had brought about recovery.

Psychotherapy is the art of helping people by listening to what they say, by encouraging them to unburden themselves of their worries. This process may not be easy for either the patient or the therapist. In the first session, the patient may well be trying to find out what sort of a person she is talking to. Can she trust him? Is he discreet? Is he really interested in her as a person? She is unlikely to talk freely until she feels confidence in her therapist. Once this is established, she is able to discuss some of her problems. She may even test him with a series of shock tactics. She is liable to turn up late for appointments to see if he will reject her, or she develops an attack of panic and sends for him out of hours. When he arrives at the house he is greeted with, "Now I know you are going to be angry with me." She may recite lurid stories, such as how at the age of thirteen she was raped by her own father, to see how the therapist responds to such a tale. If the rapport situation can survive such reactions, useful treatment is likely to emerge.

The problem may be quite easy and straightforward. A young man of twenty-six came to see me with a pain in his chest. He was convinced he had a bad heart. I knew his father had dropped dead some six months before, and I was pretty sure that the son felt he was like his father and needed reassurance on this score. The doctor has the big advantage over the lay therapist, as he can examine the man there and then and a good vetting which reveals no gross physical illness may be all the reassurance that is needed.

A young parson consulted me. He was very shy and embarrassed at first. He had had nothing to do with women most of his life. At school and university he had avoided them. At the theological college he met no women. As a parish priest he found he had to mix with them, but did not find communication at all easy. Then suddenly he met a girl his own age to whom he felt attracted. Plucking up all his courage he invited her to go out for a day to walk the hills in Derbyshire. They had a wonderful day out, but while they were having a picnic tea before coming home the young man suddenly felt he wanted to beat the girl up, to assault her. He excused himself and walked away, very upset by this curious reaction. The picnic was finally finished and he drove her home, but he found himself in quite a state. He wanted to see her again, but he was fearful of what he might do. Discussing the problem with a therapist, the explanation was fairly obvious. Never before had he spent so much time with an attractive girl on his own. During the picnic he really desired to seduce her, but this thought had so appalled him that it was censored and emerged as a desire to beat her up. In fact he did nothing, but the meaning of his reaction showed him to be a very normal young man. He was greatly reassured by talking the whole situation over, by finding the therapist could offer a reasonable explanation and was in no way surprised or shocked by his reactions.

Sexual conflicts can of course be heavily disguised. A typist came along with a shaking right hand. The shaking interfered with her efficiency at work. There was no evidence of any physical disease, and she had no major problems. She was engaged to be married but her boy friend who worked for a firm of tea importers was in India inspecting some tea gardens. They were to be married in three months when he came back.

She was asked to try and remember her dreams. At a subsequent session she said she had had a curious dream of buying a car. She got to the sales room and there were only two cars on show. One was an original T model Ford. The other was a huge 3-litre Jaguar. When asked how she recognized the Jaguar, she replied it was like the luxury model run by her boss. With very little encouragement the story became clear. She was torn between the choice of her "Tea" fiancé and the boss. Her boss was making passes at her and subconsciously she was attracted to him. She even remembered how her hand had started to shake. When she had taken him his cup of tea, he had said she should bring another cup and have one with him. Her hand shook so much she could hardly pour out the tea. After this discussion she changed her job, and her shaking hand caused her no more trouble.

Sometimes the therapist can do no more than listen and make sympathetic noises. The patient may be anxious and sick, but the problem is quite insoluble. There are many marital situations like this. A woman of forty sees me regularly to complain about her thoughtless and unkind husband. She has three children by him, but otherwise they have nothing in common, they fight whenever they meet and at times even come to blows. I have had consultations with them individually and together, and the situation seems hopeless. If there was no family they would separate, but there is a family. Month after month I have to listen to the tale of woe, and I feel quite impotent to help, but being able to talk to someone without being rebuffed seems to assist her in some small way. In other cases discussion may reveal problems which can be eased or even solved by a change in environment. A quick move to a new house may be the only solution to an impossible neighbour situation. With an elderly couple living alone, life might be rendered much more tolerable if regular home help service were introduced, along with meals on wheels. A middle aged pair coping with the heavy burden of a mentally subnormal child, might well find the drive and courage to carry on, if they could be relieved of their burden two or three times a year.

It is quite impossible to estimate with any degree of scientific accuracy how psychotherapy really helps patients, or to evaluate one type against another. Many patients will argue that they have been helped considerably by the treatment, but we all thrive on attention and kindness, and it may be that it is simply concern for the patient that has produced the improvement. During the last war we used to treat schizophrenics with large doses of insulin which put them into coma or near coma. After an appropriate time they were given syrup to drink, they recovered from the coma and ate a hearty breakfast. They put on weight, they looked better and felt better. Insulin was considered to be the cure for schizophrenia. In 1956 Ackner[6] and his colleagues tried a control experiment. Instead of using insulin to produce coma, the patients were given oral barbiturates, and an injection of sterile water. The patients passed into a kind of stupor after which they were given a good breakfast, and the improvement in the disease was every bit as good as with insulin treatment. It was not the drugs which had produced the improvement, but the care and attention given to each patient. Before the start of drug therapy for schizophrenia, there was little one could do to help the patient beyond custodial care. The schizophrenic, by her very nature shy and withdrawn, readily fell a victim to institutional neurosis. With new ideas about treatment, attention was focused on schizophrenics as never before, and they improved. Bickford[7, 8] had some novel ideas in the management of the worst and most disabled schizophrenics supervised by volunteer staff. With only basic tools such as a shovel and a barrow, they were asked to turn waste ground into tennis courts. This mammoth task improved them greatly. In another instance similar patients were sent by bus to another mental hospital for a couple of weeks under the supervision of volunteer nurses. Again the change of environment and the extra attention had an obvious beneficial effect on the patients.

Almost everyone, schizophrenic, neurotic, or even so-called

[6] Ackner, B., Harris, A. and Oldham, A. J. (1957). *Lancet*, **1,** 607.
[7] Bickford, J. A. R. (1954). *Lancet*, **1,** 943.
[8] Bickford, J. A. R. (1959). *Lancet*, **2,** 96.

normal person, thrives on any process which implies they become the focus of especial concern. Normally we derive our quota from the family circle, from friends at work or near our homes. If mentally ill, this attention factor is needed in therapeutic doses from social workers or from doctors, or even from psychiatrists.

Individual psychotherapy may help some cases, but this method is time consuming and it is by no means the only road to recovery. Often help is needed from more than one agency. Help may be needed from the employment exchange, the social security people, or the family doctor may be involved as well as the social worker. No matter to which branch the therapist belongs he owes it to his service, to his client and to himself to maintain good lines of communication.

When our earliest ancestors started evolving into Homo sapiens, two items more than anything else caused the big brain to come into being. Man began to use his hands, especially his thumbs, for making things, for doing precise or complicated jobs. They were no longer just used for climbing trees, gathering food, catching vermin, and scratching backs. The other item was communication. Apes communicate, but the form is very limited and primitive. Man developed speech and the whole process needed a big brain to make it possible. In the complex society in which we live communications are every bit as important as they ever were, but they are frequently neglected. This can happen between the adviser and patient, and between professional colleagues. The young doctor tends to be more interested in the latest technique in medicine than the more mundane and time consuming occupation of listening to what the patient has to say, and yet as Spence pointed out this basic consultation is the most important part of medicine. Social and medical services are there to help patients and people in need and many different branches may be involved over one person or one family. Lines of communication between various parts of the service are of vital importance if the machine is to work smoothly.

There are, in fact, three main methods of maintaining good

lines of communication. In order of efficiency they are as follows:

1. Face to face consultations.
2. Telephone conversations.
3. Postal communications.

FACE TO FACE MEETINGS

Face to face meetings are always the best, whether it is the general practitioner discussing a social problem with a health visitor or whether he is accompanying a consultant on a domiciliary visit. In these circumstances misunderstandings are rare, and useful information can be exchanged both ways. One afternoon I was busy writing when the front door bell rang and I found a young woman on the doorstep who introduced herself as Dr. X's health visitor. A problem family had moved into our village out of the area covered by Dr. X, and in order to achieve a smooth change-over she felt it was best to call and see me. Her diplomacy was rewarded. I was led to believe that a difficult but needy family had been passed into my care instead of feeling nettled at being landed with yet another batch of hopeless morons from a nearby community. Here in a matter of a few minutes a barrier was removed and good lines of communication were established. In the delicate world of interpersonal relationships, personal contact between the parties involved is really essential, and great care must be taken in establishing the situation with a stranger.

The first step in any interview must, in fact, be to establish a good relationship. If the consultation is with a patient, she may well be fearful and suspicious, and it may take quite a time, or even more than one interview to put her at her ease. If she is rushed, or bombarded with questions, she may well dry up and nothing useful will come out of the session. The therapist must be friendly, calm and unhurried. The patient must be told what the interview is all about, and how the therapist is trying to help. Kept in ignorance of what is going on, the patient may well panic. A group of us evolved a questionnaire for depressed patients to complete on their own in a side room. We were very proud of this tool which we felt was standardized, and to a large extent cut out the influence of the doctor in taking a history direct from the patient. It also saved a lot of time. On one occasion when I interviewed the patient after the completion of the form, I found him very worried and upset. He asked me rather fearfully if I was going to send him away. Clearly he felt that I was about to "certify" him. Forms can be very useful especially in research projects, but from the patient's angle they are not as good as the face to face contacts, and before the patient is subjected to any form, or even a questionnaire which is completed by the social worker, care must be taken to see that a good rapport has been established, and that the patient knows what is happening. If the form is not too detailed, it is better to complete it after the interview. If it must be filled in on the spot, the patient deserves an apology as well as an explanation. If care is not taken to prepare the patient and win her confidence, the interview becomes comparable with a police interrogation, and the patient grows more and more hostile. Little good will come from such a contact. Long interviews may be looked on as routine by caseworkers, but they can be very wearing indeed for the patient, and care must be taken to see that she is not becoming too exhausted, or worried because she had promised to meet the children from school half an hour before. Splendid work can be done by long interviews but the worker must be very skilled. An experienced psychiatric social worker once spent some weeks in this practice interviewing the family of every epileptic. The parents of the patient were warned beforehand and given the opportunity to refuse such an interview. Such was the skill of this worker that in no time she was viewed as a friend of the family, and questions which had worried the parents just poured out. Several people told me how useful the long sessions had been. This was indeed a research project, but the social worker knew her job, and on each occasion established such a good rapport that the interviews were therapeutic as well as being the occasion for collecting research data. The care of the patient must always be more important than the collection of facts, and the worker who is collecting data must feel that the job is interesting and worthwhile. Form filling by passive disinterested workers is unlikely to achieve any worthwhile results, and it is hard luck on the patient who is unlikely to benefit in any way by the procedure.

Knowing a person by name adds some extra meaning or intimacy to the interview, and it is essential if there is going to be a useful relationship between people. The almost mystical significance of a name is described in the Bible, when after the disaster of the golden calf incident, Moses entered the tabernacle to plead with God for the Jews. "The Lord spake unto Moses face to face," we are told, "As a man speaketh unto his friend." During the same conversation the Almighty had said to him "I know thee by name," thereby sealing both the importance and the intimacy of the interview. Most banks and big stores have got the message, and large labels indicate the name of the teller or the saleswoman. Labels are very important because, even if the social worker introduces himself, the householder may be in a state of embarrassment or confusion and the name is soon forgotten, and it takes courage to ask the question "What did you say your name was?" Anybody visiting people in their homes professionally should surely be able to give them a card, giving both their name and their status, and in these days of large partnerships and rotas it would improve communication if this applied to doctors as well as social workers. Within the office or surgery names should be on desks or labels clearly legible should be worn. Just wearing a label is not enough, the lettering must be large enough to be read without peering, something most of us would be too shy to do. Finally if the name is too difficult for people to remember, then a simplified version should be used for professional purposes. If a Miss Jones marries a Pole called Boris Szczurowski, she would be wise to practise under her maiden name, or use his forename and be Mrs. Boris. Mrs. Boris is much more likely to be remembered than Mrs. Szczurowska. This all sounds so obvious and yet time and again I am told by patients that "a woman called" to see about getting Grandma into a home for a few days. They have no idea who she was, and she has left no tangible evidence of her visit. It is quite exceptional to be told that Mrs. Smith of the social services department called to help and sort out some social problem, but this approach makes a much better impression on the family.

One final word on techniques in interviews. It is of great importance to use the most simple language and to choose words that the patient will be able to understand even when under stress. Doctors are probably more guilty than most other workers of using long and technical words. It is so easy for patients to misinterpret what they hear and to think the worst. A year or so ago there was a rabies scare in the South of England. A woman consulted her doctor about her small girl. They had had a case of rabies at the nursery school and she understood you could get it from a mere scratch. Incredulous, the general practitioner rang the director of the school. They had in fact a case of scabies! A woman with a patch of unpigmented skin on her arm burst into tears as she showed it to me. One of my partners had quite correctly called it leucoderma. She had heard leukaemia, and hence her despair. In dealing with people and their emotional or social problems, it is of the utmost importance that both sides should speak the same language, but this is much more difficult to accomplish than it sounds.

TELEPHONE COMMUNICATIONS

Telephone communications can be very useful indeed, or things can become very distorted, depending on how the parties know each other. If a welfare worker rings me up and we know each other and have worked together in the past, the chances are that we have learned to speak the same language, and in such circumstances the telephone contact can be as useful as the face to face consultation. On the other hand if I have to ring up the hospital about an admission, and I speak to a young houseman, our contact may not be quite so rewarding. We are both highly suspicious of each other. I feel that he hoards beds as a miser hoards money. He feels that I am trying to put one across him and get rid of an awkward patient. The gulf, one might almost say the enmity, between the young houseman and the general practitioner is traditional and to some extent understandable. The work and the backgrounds of the two parties are poles apart; each cherishes a somewhat caricatured picture of the other, and there is little chance to improve the relationship by personal contact, and so the wrangle over hospital admissions goes on. If by any chance I do meet the young doctor face to face and we get to know each other, the atmosphere changes at once.

Telephone contacts are, in fact, both useful and time saving. Some doctors reserve half an hour before surgery during which time they are available on the phone to patient or colleague direct. At other times they are buffered from outside calls by a secretary or a wife, so that some of the work can be filtered off. In an emergency, if the doctor is at home, he should always be available. I find it hard to understand why some general practitioners hide behind an ex-directory number. This strange habit has become almost universal and is bad for our image, not only among patients but also with colleagues, and it is so unnecessary. If not on call the doctor can avoid answering the phone himself. Whoever picks up the receiver says he is engaged, and never that he is out, and nine times out of ten can deal with the problem, but if he is needed the doctor himself can take over. I do not suppose this happens more than once a month in our practice, and I often find I can help with very little trouble, where a stranger to the problem would be in difficulties. For example a patient might be worried by symptoms which were clearly side effects of a drug I had prescribed. I could reassure the patient or readjust the dosage quite simply. On very rare occasions there are different reasons for my intervention. One night when another member of the rota was on call there was a message that a child had been killed in one of our villages. It is hard indeed to find any means to console in this situation, but the family doctor who knows the people concerned is in a far better position to help than any stranger.

This whole question of ex-directory numbers must be very

frustrating for consultants who wish to contact the general practitioner out of hours about a patient they may have just seen, as talks like this can be most useful. I feel very strongly about this gimmick, which is as wrong as it is unnecessary. Busy general practitioners are unlikely to be available except during surgery hours, or after the day's work, and people are often very diffident about using either of these times. If a short talk is all that is necessary there need be no hesitation and if a longer chat is necessary it is always possible to ask when it will be convenient. Having accepted a time for the talk it is important to ring punctually. I am never available between 11.00 a.m. and 1.00 p.m. for instance, and callers are invited to ring during the lunch break at 1.00 p.m. for half an hour. It is a bit irritating for all concerned if they ring at 2.00 p.m. when I have had to start on my rounds again.

COMMUNICATION BY LETTER

Once again, if one knows the writer, misunderstandings are much less likely to occur. The big advantage of the written word is that one has a dated record, and this does not apply to the other forms of communication. The great danger is that the letter gets pushed into the pending file and forgotten. It would seem to me that there was a great setback to the art of letter writing stemming from the postal strike of 1971. The postal service itself is slower and less efficient and those who write letters seem less able or willing to communicate. Letters can be too long or too short, and one which covers more than one side of quarto paper has to be very good indeed to be read with any profit or pleasure. Morrison[9] went even further in the condemnation of long letters. He suggested that a law should be passed limiting letters to one side of a sheet of paper, and the letter should be written in such a style that any eight year old could understand it. In days gone by hospital consultants were quite rightly thoroughly irritated by the so-called letter on a visiting card, with

[9] Morrison, M. (1973). *World Medicine*, January, p. 11.

the words "Has he a chest? Please see and advise." The classical answer was well deserved : "Has chest."

The unanswered letter is probably the most tiresome of all. Surely any first letter deserves a prompt answer of some sort, if only to say the letter has been received. If I write to the Social Services office about some problem, I want to know that they have received my letter, that something is being done, or the matter referred elsewhere. A first class job may be done by trained social workers, but if I do not know what they are doing I am left feeling frustrated. There are of course many problems these workers can do without any reference to the general practitioner but, if the latter is in any way involved, he should be kept informed. In the same way if the general practitioner has to hospitalize, as an emergency, some person already under the care of other workers, it is only good manners to see that all the parties are informed. It is thoroughly irritating to say the least, for a district nurse to make an early morning call on an elderly diabetic, only to find she has been moved to hospital during the night, and exasperating for a social worker to discover that all her arrangements for a family have been thrown into confusion because the mother has been sent into hospital with appendicitis, and no one has bothered to tell her what has happened.

CONCLUSION

We all pay lip service to the importance of good lines of communication, but when it comes to practical measures, our performance often falls far short of our good intentions. A tape recording of telephone conversations could be very revealing and chastening. The speaker often does not realize how he or she bristles when a call comes at some inconvenient moment and how abrupt and offputting the response has become. There are times when we are overworked and under stress and it is then that we are most likely to react in such a way that our patients do not say what they wanted to say, and the consultation is wasted. When a letter arrives criticizing some view or action we have taken, the natural response is to write an aggressive letter in return, and the lines of communication are thereby rendered pretty useless for a long time to come.

Each of us is the member of a team, and we are all experts in our own field. To get the best out of our efforts we must work together as a team, and this can only be done if there are good lines of communication. They must be good enough, and the workers must know each other well enough, to be able to disagree without offence. The success or failure of the health service and the social services depends more than anything else on the good relationships and lines of communication between the various branches of the service, and between us and our clients. If we do not make it clear by the way we talk and the way we behave that we are interested in people and are keen to help them in their trouble, we are largely wasting our time.

There is a desperate need for more help in the battle against the blue plague, and every section of the community has a part to play. We need all the assistance the psychiatric services can give, we need better trained family doctors. We need to make use of all the skills of the trained social workers, and all the well directed enthusiasm of community organizations such as Darby and Joan Clubs, the Samaritans, and the like. There is a place for the kindness of the good neighbour, the skill of the psychotherapist, the effectiveness of modern drugs and techniques. For the few in serious trouble the hospital bed or day hospital facilities are a temporary respite from the battle of life which for a time has proved overwhelming. Social workers, doctors and their drugs, and voluntary helpers all have their place, but we must never lose sight of the ultimate goal for each patient. The best treatment of all is that which reinstates the patient, stands him on his own feet and renders him independent of all outside aids.

Glossary

DELUSION   A false belief not susceptible to argument or reason.

DELIRIUM TREMENS   A state of excitement and confusion with disorientation, and vivid hallucinations due to acute or chronic alcoholism.

DEMENTIA   A form of mental disorder in which the cognitive and intellectual functions of the mind are affected. Loss of memory is a prominent symptom. The illness implies some degree of permanent change.

EMPATHY   The ability to enter into and understand the emotional state of another person.

EUPHORIA   A bodily sense of wellbeing and comfort.

FUNCTIONAL   Connected with the function of an organ but not involving the structure; it has come to mean psychic rather than somatic in reference to a symptom.

HALLUCINATION   The subjective experience of a perception in the absence of a corresponding percept in the external real world. These can occur with any of the senses, but the most common are auditory or visual.

HOMEOSTASIS   The condition of bodily equilibrium, as in mood or body temperature.

HORMONE   Any substance secreted by a ductless gland into the blood stream, where it is carried to some other organ to stimulate some activity.

HYPOCHONDRIASIS   A state of mind in which the person is preoccupied with his health, so that he can think of little else. No physical cause for the symptoms can be found.

HYPOMANIA   An exaggerated feeling of wellbeing, with overactivity and a tendency to talk, but not amounting to true mania.

HYPNOTIC A drug which induces sleep.

HYPOTHALAMUS That part of the brain below the thalamus which integrates and controls autonomic functions.

NEUROSIS An illness of the personality, manifested as a functional derangement of the mind or body. The victim usually has insight into her condition.

PARANOIA A state of mind in which the patient tends to have a persecution complex, and little or no insight into her problem.

REPRESSION The active rejection of unacceptable ideas or instinctual impulses, so that they are forced from consciousness into the unconscious.

SCHIZOPHRENIA A mental disorder with some disintegration of the personality. There is an impaired relationship with reality, hallucinations and delusions can occur.

SUBCONSCIOUS That part of the mind containing mental processes not present in consciousness at any given moment, yet available to introspection.

Some Useful Addresses

The Abbeyfield Society, 22 Nottingham Place, LONDON W1M 3FB (01-935 0751).

Homes for elderly and lonely old people.

AGE CONCERN. National Old People's Welfare Council, 55 Gower St., LONDON WC1E 6HJ (01-637 2886).

Problems connected with old people.

The Albany Trust, 32 Shaftesbury Avenue, LONDON W1V 8EP. (01-734 5588).

Works to promote psychological health, currently working on problems of homosexuality.

ALCOHOLISM. National Council on Alcoholism, Hope House, 45 Great Peter St., Westminster, LONDON, S.W.1 (01-222 1056/7).

For any advice on alcoholism, by victims or relatives.

Alcoholics Anonymous, 11 Redcliffe Gardens, LONDON, S.W.10.

Self help society of ex-alcoholics designed to help those in trouble.

Church Army Counselling Centre, 5 Cosway St., LONDON, N.W.1 (01-262 0756).

Help for all in trouble. Homes for aged and lonely people.

CITIZEN'S ADVICE BUREAUX. National Citizen's Advice Bureaux Council, 26 Bedford Square, LONDON WC1B 3HU (01-636 4066).

C.A.B. Offices can be found in all large towns.

CRUSE, The Charter House, 6 Lion Gate Gardens, Richmond, Surrey TW9 2DF (01-940 2660).

The organization for widows and their children.

FAMILY PLANNING ASSOCIATION, Margaret Pyke House, 27-35 Mortimer Street, LONDON W1A 4QW (01-636 7866).

All problems concerned with contraception, subfertility and sexual problems.

MARIE CURIE MEMORIAL FOUNDATION, 124 Sloane Street, LONDON SW1X 9BP (01-730 9157).

For the welfare of those suffering from cancer, and help in nursing during the terminal stages.

MARRIAGE GUIDANCE COUNCIL, The National Marriage Guidance Council, 3 Gower Street, LONDON WC1E 6HA (01-935 2838).

All problems dealing with marriage and sex.

MIND, The National Association for Mental Health, 39 Queen Anne St., LONDON W1M 0AJ (01-935 1272).

Problems dealing with mental illnesses of all kinds.

RED CROSS, British Red Cross Society, 14-15 Grosvenor Cres., LONDON, S.W.1.

There are Red Cross Centres in all big towns. For very small fees all kinds of useful aids can be hired or bought.

SAMARITANS, The Samaritans, St. Stephen Walbrook, 39 Walbrook, LONDON EC4N 8BP (01-626 2277. Emergency 01-626 9000).

To befriend the suicidal and despairing. There are Samaritan organizations in every big town.

SINGLE WOMEN, The National Council for the Single Woman and her Dependants, 166 Victoria Street, LONDON SW1 (01-828 5511).

To promote the welfare of single women with family responsibilities.

S.O.S. The S.O.S. Society, 14 Culford Gardens, LONDON SW3 2SU (01-584 3717/8).

Hostels for young men and students in London, a mental after-care hostel for men and women; homes for old people, hostels for temporarily homeless men.

Index